The Construction of a European Community

Achievements and Prospects for the Future

PRAEGER SPECIAL STUDIES IN INTERNATIONAL ECONOMICS AND DEVELOPMENT

Praeger Publishers   New York   London

Library of Congress Cataloging in Publication Data

Maillet, Pierre, economist.
  The construction of a European Community.

  (Praeger special studies in international economics
and development)
  Translation of La construction européenne.
  Bibliography: p.
  1. European Economic Community. 2. European
Economic Community countries—Foreign economic
relations. I. Title.
HC241.2.M23613   1977   341.24'2   77-10605
ISBN 0-03-022366-0

Originally published in French as *La Construction Européenne*
© 1975 Presses Universitoires de France

PRAEGER SPECIAL STUDIES
200 Park Avenue, New York, N.Y., 10017, U.S.A.

Published in the United States of America in 1977
by Praeger Publishers,
A Division of Holt, Rinehart and Winston, CBS, Inc.

789 038 987654321

English translation © 1977 by Praeger Publishers

Printed in the United States of America

CONTENTS

LIST OF TABLES AND FIGURE

Table   Page

Table | Page

Figure

On March 25, 1957, Belgium, Germany, France, Italy, Luxembourg and The Netherlands signed the Treaty of Rome setting up the European Economic Community (EEC). The EEC's purpose was defined in these terms:

> The Community shall have as its task, by establishing a common market and progressively drawing together the economic policies of the Member States, to promote throughout the Community a harmonious development of economic activities, a continuous and balanced expansion, an increase in stability, an accelerated raising of the standard of living, and closer relations between the states belonging to it.

For 15 years, the EEC countries have easily figured among the leaders in terms of economic growth. The gross national product (GNP) at constant prices of the Community has doubled, with an average increase of 5.5 percent per annum. This is a slightly higher rate than that of the years before 1958, particularly in Belgium and The Netherlands. This rise in output has gone hand in hand with an increase in per capita income and consumption. Taking into account a 12 percent increase in the Community's population, the rise in the per capita GNP was 73 percent, or 4.5 percent per year. As of 1973, the EEC countries ranked among the richest countries in the world, with its three leading members coming second only to the United States, Canada, Australia, Sweden, and Switzerland.[*]

Therefore, as stipulated in the Treaty, there has been continuous expansion and a rise in the standard of living. But this fact raises two questions: Is the economic growth experienced by EEC members a result of Community construction? And if so, have they reaped what they hoped to sow?

Interesting in themselves, these questions take on special importance if two major events of 1973 are considered: the widening of the EEC to include three new partners (the United Kingdom, Denmark, and Ireland) and the crisis following the massive price increases of petroleum at the end of 1973. Not having taken part in

---

[*] General statistics on the EEC are given in the table at the end of this introduction.

the Community experiment and often having political and economic problems that are different from those of the other six, the three new partners have been led to question the validity of certain basic conceptions. Even if in signing the membership treaty they have committed themselves to making the EEC experience their own, this questioning is only natural and could turn out to be very profitable if carried on in a positive frame of mind. Indeed, the international situation has changed a great deal in 15 years, and even more so in the last three, as well as the aspirations of the different populations. What were once valid solutions may now need modifying, and new approaches must be found immediately.

However, in redefining a Community course of action, we must not disregard what the past has taught us. On the contrary, it is only in examining what has worked well and what has worked less well that we will be able to give any new decisions their maximum effectiveness.

The object of this book, therefore, is to analyze what has been accomplished in the past 15 years, to seek out the causes of the successes and the failures, and, from these, to deduce a course of action for the future.

Historically, European construction has been motivated by a series of political, cultural, and economic reasons.

The political reasons are fairly clear. The point was, and still is, to give the European continent enough importance to make her voice heard in the global dialogue along with the other great powers; to hold a political position at the international level sought by the European people; and to play an effective part in the gradual world construction. *

Equally important are the cultural reasons (in the largest sense of the word). Many Europeans are of the opinion that the European culture heritage has intrinsic worth and that, without systematically taking a stand against other countries or continents, a specific European character should be preserved when confronted by the threat of domination by other cultures, whether they come from the East or from the West.

Last but not least are the economic considerations, which are the main subject of this book; however, it should always be kept in

---

* To be more clear, it should be noted that these reasons gradually emerged during the 1950s and led to the signing of the Treaty of Rome. But underlying Robert Schuman's statement on May 9, 1950, which, in turn, led to the signing of the Treaty of Paris (which set up the European Coal and Steel Community), was the wish for a Franco-German reconciliation. This has been very clearly explained by the initiator of the whole matter, Jean Monnet, in his Mémoires. [1]

mind that they are not the only considerations and should in no way be thought of as the primary objective in building Europe.

By far the major concern is the search for efficiency: the attempt to profit from the lower production costs made possible by specialization and the savings due to large-scale production without losing the favorable effect of competition among several manufacturers for the same market. Likewise, the EEC can bank on a greater variety of products being made available to the consumer, and finally, there is the hope to have better control over the ups and downs of the economy.

While promoting efficiency, economic integration should facilitate the pursuit of other goals of a more social nature, such as furthering the growth of regions that have lagged behind and raising the living conditions of the most underprivileged social groups of the population.

Thus, the economic union of several countries may be thought of as a "nonzero sum game." Here, any "surpluses" yielded by this union might be divided up among the various member countries, each profiting from its participation in the whole. But we might go a step further and imagine turning over this "surplus" primarily to the least wealthy countries and, in doing so, carry over to the Community level an idea of "solidarity," now being practiced to a certain degree on the national level between various regions and which is the basis of regional policies.

To attain the following goals, our foreign trade, favored by the setting up of a free trade area, where the movement of goods should be unimpeded, is already invaluable, but insufficient.

1. Not only must goods circulate, but the units of production must be situated for optimum efficiency, whereas now, the best distribution of the factors of production is thwarted by a series of regulatory and fiscal differences.

2. Moreover, the centuries have shown that borders open one day may close again; in order to avert this, there must be real interpenetration of economies.

But if the building of a real common market provides the answer, at least in part, to these concerns, it can only be a transitional stage. Actually, the various states intervene in the running of the national economies, on a large scale. Furthermore, the economic opening of the borders has made the economic situation of one country more sensitive to that of another. Out of this arises a twofold need to coordinate, and sometimes to unite, public efforts at intervention in the economy and, at the same time, to guarantee a minimum of harmonization in economic developments.

This need for harmonization requires going beyond the Common Market and constructing a real economic union, which would be reflected by a degree of agreement on economic policies. It was the recognition of this necessity to go beyond the simple setting-up of a free trade area that led the member countries of the EEC to establish Community institutions, to provide them with the necessary means of action, and to accept the transfer of jurisdiction from the national authorities to these Community institutions. We will see that the Community is endowed with institutions of a profoundly original nature.

The executive is a double-headed executive. The Commission ensures that the provisions of the Treaty are respected. It may make decisions in certain areas (limited) set by the Treaty, but, above all, it has as its basic function the formulating of recommendations. The Council is the essential deciding body, but, as a general rule, may only vote on motions put forward by the Commission. The Parliament exercises a certain political supervision, which remains for the moment rather restricted. The Court of Justice hears cases and settles legal disputes brought before it by the governments, by the Commission, by corporations, or by private individuals.

The two basic organs are, therefore, the Commission and the Council. In fact, the system can only work if there is trust and close cooperation between them, which presupposes a political willingness on the part of each government to continue on the road to integration.

For those areas that are not left totally in the hands of national or local administrations, the Community institutions can act in three main ways (if we go beyond the simple exchange of information): in order of increasing integration, they are consultation, coordination, or common policy.

A true formal consultation means that before making decisions, a government is required to ask the opinion of the Community institutions and its partners about its plans. This is a way of seeing that the projects as a whole of each government are consistent. Strictly speaking, the advice need not be followed but on a practical level, this exchange of opinions may lead the country to alter its planning.

The coordination option goes much further, as this leads to decisions binding upon every country. This makes it possible to ensure that the measures actually taken in each country are all consistent since they were decided together (either by majority vote or unanimously).

However, if decisions are made as a group, putting them into force stays at the national level. The coordination aspect therefore respects national borders, and the nature and scope of the measures taken may differ from one country to the next.

Common policy is the most integrated of all the institutional powers. Once decided for the whole of the Community, it abolishes all borders. Setting up Community institutions with certain powers makes it necessary to grant them certain jurisdictions, which are thus withdrawn from the national governments. If one looks at the instruments of economic policy formerly in the hands of the governments, one finds that one of the four following possibilities holds true:

1. The jurisdiction of the national authorities has not changed; Community institutions do not intervene in the national use of this instrument (they can, however, superimpose a Community course of action over the national one—the clearest example is the Social Fund).

2. The national jurisdiction is slightly reduced because of the exchange of views between members that is provided for (a simple exchange of information, followed by official discussions or official consultation).

3. The national jurisdiction is restricted, either because it is necessary to coordinate or bring into line the activities of the member countries in a certain field or because Commission authorization is needed.

4. National jurisdiction is totally eliminated; decision-making power belongs to Community institutions (either according to the general procedure—a motion made by the Commission or a decision taken by the Council—or according to the special procedure of the Commission in those cases provided for by the Treaty or where power has been delegated by the Council).

Last, one must not overlook the pre-eminence of Community law over national law.

The following table shows the theoretical division of powers as provided for by the different treaties. We are aware that there is sometimes a certain divergence between the letter of a Treaty and the way it is applied. Obviously, the transfer of national jurisdiction to European institutions has raised—or continues to raise—problems so thorny that they slow down the completion of this transfer. On the other hand, on certain points, the evolution of the Community has gone further than the letter of the treaties prescribed.

To sum up, Community construction is following five major lines of force:

1. the creation of European economic territory, by eliminating those artificial elements that have acted to create differences above and beyond the national ones;

Powers Of The National Governments Transferred To The Community Institutions

Instruments	Powers of the National Authorities	Role Played by the Community Institutions	
		Influence on Decisions Made at the National Level	Decisions by the Community
Public Finances			
Operating expenses	Unchanged (but no discrimination among suppliers)	Directives (or proposals for directives) on the procedures for making public tenders	
Public investments	Slightly changed (exchanges of views)	Attempts at coordination, particularly in transport and energy	
Transfers to individuals	Unchanged (provided that there is no discrimination among nationals of the various countries)		Social Fund
Operating subsidies to firms	Limited (with review by the Commission)	Checks to see if they are compatible with the Common Market (Articles 92 and 93)	EAGGF (European Agricultural Guidance and Guarantee Fund).
Capital subsidies	Limited (with review by the Commission)	Checks to see if they are compatible with the Common Market (Articles 92 and 93)	The Commission proposed industrial development contracts
Transfers to the rest of the world	Unchanged		EDF (European Development Fund).
Indirect taxes	Limited: discriminatory taxes forbidden (Articles 95 to 98); the remission of charges are reviewed (Articles 92 & 93); general setting up of the value added tax (VAT) system (decision made on the basis of Article 99).	Assures that there is no discrimination and verifies the remission of charges. Proposals for harmonization (based on Article 99) (attempts at alignment of VAT rates)	European Coal and Steel Community (ECSC) levy. Own resources (Treaty of April 22, 1970)

Direct taxes on private income	Unchanged	Proposals for harmonization (based on Article 99)	
Direct taxes on corporate income	Unchanged		
Customs duties: intra-Community; nonmember countries	Abolished: duties eliminated on July, 1968 Abolished: the common external tariff put into effect on July, 1968 (with special provisions for the Associated States and Greece and generalized preferences to the less developed countries starting July, 1971)		Fixing of the External Common Tariff and the rates of agricultural levies
Social Security contributions	Unchanged	Social Security system for migrant workers	
Property and inheritance taxes	Unchanged		
Transfers from the rest of the world	Unchanged		
Loans to firms	Limited (in those forms that might constitute State aids, Articles 92 and 93)	Checked to see if they are compatible with the Common Market	
Loans to the rest of the world	Unchanged		
Internal borrowings	Unchanged		ECSC loans EIB (European Investment Bank) loans
Borrowings from the rest of the world: intra-Community; nonmember countries	Unchanged Unchanged		The ECSC and the EIB may borrow on the markets of member countries and nonmember countries
Balance of current transactions	Slightly changed	Council opinion on economic policy	
Balance of revenue and expenditure	Slightly changed	Council opinion on economic policy	

| Instruments | Powers of the National Authorities | Role Played by the Community Institutions | |
		Influence on Decisions Made at the National Level	Decisions by the Community
Regulations Acting Directly on Certain Economic Parameters			
A. Money, currency, and credit			
Direct monetary instruments (rediscount rates, open market operations, and so forth)	Slightly changed	Coordination attempts (Monetary Committee, Economic Policy Committee, Committee of the Governors of the central banks)	
Regulation of bank credit	Slightly changed	Coordination attempts (Monetary Committee, Economic Policy Committee, Committee of the Governors of the central banks)	
Regulation of capital operations	Unchanged		
Control over exchanges: in regard to member countries; in regard to nonmember countries	Abolished	May be authorized by the Commission	
B. Other regulations acting directly on certain economic parameters			
Price regulation	Limited—abolished for coal, steel, and agricultural produce		Fixing of agricultural prices, review of the scale of charges filed by iron and steel producers.
Wage regulation	Limited; all discrimination based on nationality forbidden (Article 48); equal pay for men and women (Article 119)		
Changing of the exchange rate	Limited (prior consultation required)		

Regulation of imports and exports, trade agreements: intra-Community and with nonmember countries	Abolished (free movement Abolished (common commercial policy)		Common Commercial Policy worked out Negotiations with nonmember countries
Institutional or Regulatory Framework			
System of property	Unchanged		
Commercial laws	Slightly changed (attempts at alignment)	Directives for the approximation of provisions that directly affect the functioning of the Common Market (Article 100)	
Rules of competition	Slightly changed by the pre-eminence of Community rules		Ensures that articles 85 and 86 are applied
Regulation of working conditions	Limited: all discrimination based on nationality forbidden (Article 48); equivalence between paid holiday schemes maintained (Article 120)	Studies and opinions to promote close cooperation	
Technical regulations	Limited	Directives to eliminate technical obstacles to trade (Article 100)	
Regulation of immigration: member countries;	Abolished: free movement of paid labor; freedom of establishment		
nonmember countries	Unchanged		
Economic Information	Unchanged	Medium-Term Program	Statistical Office of the European Communities

The EEC, the United States, and the World: General Statistics, 1974

Country	Area	Population in Millions	Population Density km²	GDP 10⁹ km² units of account*	Investments in Percentage of GDP	Active Population		
						In Agriculture	In Industry	In Services
EEC	1,528	257.8	169	918	22.8	8.9	42.6	48.5
Germany	249	62.0	250	305	22.8	7.3	47.6	45.1
France	547	52.5	96	213	25.1	12.0	39.2	49.2
Italy	301	55.4	184	120	23.4	16.6	44.1	39.3
Netherlands	41	13.5	332	55	22.2	6.6	35.5	57.9
Belgium	30	9.8	320	42	22.7	3.7	41.2	55.1
Luxembourg	3	0.4	137	2	25.5	6.6	49.0	44.4
United Kingdom	244	56.1	230	151	20.1	2.8	42.3	54.9
Ireland	70	3.1	44	5	24.7	24.3	31.1	44.6
Denmark	43	5.0	117	25	21.9	9.6	32.3	58.1
United States	9,363	211.9	23	1,118	17.5	4.1	31.7	64.2
World	135,897	3,890.0	—	—	—	—	—	—

*In 1974, one unit of account equaled $ 1.25.

The EEC Compared with the World
(percent)

Factors	EEC	United States	USSR
Area	1.1	6.8	16.5
Population	6.6	5.5	6.5
Estimated GDP	27	33	15
Energy consumption	16.3	31.5	15.7
Energy production	6.3	25.3	18.9
Foreign trade (excluding intra-EEC trade)	22.5	14.7	3.9

2. determined intervention in the structures of production, either by means of prohibition (competition policy) or by means of stimulation;
3. an action that aims at reorienting the spontaneous evolution in the distribution of incomes or the use to which the GNP is put;
4. a policy that aims at ensuring stable expansion; and
5. a foreign policy toward other developed countries and the developing countries.

These are the five topics to be examined in the five following chapters.

NOTE

1. Jean Monnet, Mémoires (Paris: Eayard, 1976).

IS THE COMMUNITY A
UNIFIED ECONOMIC AREA?

After more than 15 years of European construction, it is only right to ask whether the Community now forms an integrated economic area. The answer may be sought either in assessing to what degree the arbitrary differentiating factors have been eliminated or by observing the results of the behavior of economic agents, particularly in matters of trade and prices. These two approaches will be applied one after the other.

If the first approach is applied, it will show whether the obstacles to trade and the movement of the factors of production have been done away with and if legal or statutory disparities have been lessened.

There are three acid tests for the existence of a unified economic area: the trend toward a single price system throughout the territory; the expansion of the trade between regions in this area; and the transformation of the structures of production. Only the first two points will be tackled here; the third will be the subject of Chapter 2.

PREREQUISITES TO UNIFICATION

By unified economic area, essentially what is meant is an area where decisions to buy goods and services and where to situate the units of production are made in such a way that the location of the producer of goods and services and the sites of the units of production are not influenced by current political borders or economic differences other than those resulting from geographic differences and the legacy of history, particularly as far as the state of the substructures and the actual state of territorial development go.

1

The conditions necessary to establish such an area are listed
in the Treaty, particularly in Part Two under Article I (Common
Rules) of Part Three. They include the following items:

the prohibition of customs duties on imports and exports or any
    charges having an equivalent effect (Article 9);
the adoption of a common customs tariff in their relations with
    countries outside the Common Market (third countries) (Article
    9);
the opening of public markets to outside suppliers;
the harmonization of taxation (Article 99);
a common transport policy (Article 74);
the freedom of establishment (Article 52);
unrestricted providing of services (Article 59);
the freedom of movements of capital (Article 67);
freedom of movement for workers (Article 48);
the rules of competition applying to undertakings (agreements on
    restrictive practices and use of a dominant position) (Articles
    85 and 86);
the supervision of aid granted by the state (Article 92); and
approximation of laws (Article 100).

The degree to which these different conditions have been met
is very uneven. This will now be seen in a quick survey of the first
eight points (leaving the others for later chapters).
All tariff-related obstacles to the movement of goods were
totally eliminated by July, 1968, at the time the common customs
tariff was set up. However, a series of nontariff-related obstacles
have remained. Because of these, many tasks have to be accomplished
before the customs union becomes a reality, such as the elimination
of those remaining charges that act like customs duties and the
harmonization of the customs legislation of the different countries.
Moreover, although following its course, the completion of
the general program to eliminate all technical hindrances to trade
resulting from the diversity of legislative, statutory, and administrative regulations of the member states is far off. Although it seems
that, with exceptions, such diversity does not set serious obstacles
to the flow of trade, nevertheless, by raising production costs, it
brings about economic waste that is all the more regrettable because
often there are no objective reasons for this diversity. It is estimated
that several more years will be necessary before the goal can be
reached. But in order to accomplish this, it is not enough to get
rid of the existing obstacles; it is also necessary to avoid creating
new ones, and, therefore, it will be required to keep in line all new
technical regulations necessitated by technological developments

(such as the appearance of new products) or by changes in behavior
and public opinion (a stricter approach to pollution, and so forth)
throughout the Community.

As for the public tenders, it was stipulated in the Treaty that
all discriminatory practice would become illegal by the end of the
transition period. Yet, a recent message sent to the Council by the
Commission has shown that the current situation is far from that
foreseen by the Treaty. Whereas a real advance for the traditional
markets of standard supplies is expected in a short time, Community
trade in capital goods and so-called high-technology products has
stayed low, and even insignificant, in the case of power stations and
telecommunications equipment. Keeping public tenders partitioned
prevents the buyer from profiting from the competition between
firms and also prevents the firms from going further in the specialization needed to manufacture these same goods with economies of
scale.

The practices concerning public tenders must be completely
revised; it is necessary to ban all discrimination on national grounds.
At the present time, governments display an understandable unwillingness to cease favoring their own manufacturers for reasons of
employment, regional stability, national defense, and, often, prestige.
One way to proceed might be to come to an agreement on throwing
open public tenders by stages, with each stage including products of
interest to the producers of the various countries, making possible
a balanced progression.

The Commission has gone further, by proposing an actual union
of public tenders. It is an interesting idea, at least for those products
where very advanced standardization and the grouping of orders on a
very small number of machines make it possible to reap sizable
economies of scale. Yet, care must be taken not to let this gain be
canceled out, or worse, by the loss of information and stimulus to
innovation that may result from the different experiences of various
buyers. This is particularly important in sectors where technology
evolves rapidly, where a balance must be maintained between an
excessive pace of innovation and one that is too slow. In the former
case, the producer may not be able to redeem his research and
development costs or his investments on "long runs" and may entail
costly outlay on new techniques. In the latter case, he may not be able
to use new technological discoveries to the fullest.

Tax disparities existing between countries trying to set up a
common market raise two types of problems: on one hand, they may
distort competition between producers from different countries selling
on the same national market; on the other hand, they may stand in the
way of using the factors of production most efficiently. At the outset,
there were substantial differences among the tax systems of the

countries (whereas the overall tax rate varied little from country to country): the two major differences consisted, on one hand, in the amount of direct taxes compared with indirect taxes and, on the other hand, the methods of levying indirect taxes—the value added tax (VAT) in France and the cumulating turnover taxes in other countries.

The problem has become simpler since the Community countries adopted the VAT system, which replaced the earlier system of cumulating turnover taxes (the last country of the Six to adopt the VAT was Italy, on January 1, 1973, and the new Three have accepted the principle of the VAT. But as the VAT rates remain different (with very great disparities), the problem is far from solved. [*]

TABLE 1.1

Evolution of the Share of Income Taxes in the Total
Tax Receipts—Germany, France, Italy, The Netherlands,
and Belgium, 1958, 1965, and 1971

Country of Origin	1958	1965	1971
Germany	37	42	46
France	26	25	28
Italy	30	33	34
Netherlands	53	54	55
Belgium	40	41	47

Source: Statistical Office of the European Communities (SOEC).

On another hand (see Table 1.1), the cases are very different if one looks at the distribution of the tax burden between direct and indirect taxes. Even if income tax has been tending to play a greater role in all the countries, the gaps have not narrowed between France and Italy and the three other countries.

From a practical standpoint, there are three possible ways to avoid the double taxing of an exported product: the principle of taxation at place of origin (no taxation in the buying country); the principle of taxation at the place of destination (with the charges deducted on

---

[*]As of January 1, 1977, the normal VAT rates stood at 18 percent in Belgium and The Netherlands, 17.6 percent in France, 12 percent in Italy, 11 percent in Germany, and 8 percent in the United Kingdom. Moreover, there are major differences between the minimum and maximum rates, which range from 7 percent to 33 percent in France and from 0 percent to 25 percent in the United Kingdom.

leaving the producing country and reapplied on entering the buying
country); and bringing the different countries' tax rates completely
into line.

From an economic standpoint, it can be shown that the first
two solutions amount to the same thing in their effects on competition
between producers—contrary to the impression that exporters from
countries with heavy indirect taxes could suffer in relation to producers from countries with lighter indirect taxes (the exporters in
these second countries to the contrary being favored when exporting
to the first). If the rates vary, any adjustments will be made by the
exchange rate, [1] which will be different according to whether the
taxes are applied in the sending or receiving country.*

But this is only true if the tax rate is the same for all products
in each country. If not, certain products are favored and others
penalized—by the choice of one system over another. Now, a multitude of tax rates is very common in all the countries; besides the
general rate, there are reduced rates (often applied on foodstuffs)
and higher rates (for luxury goods, as well as cars in certain countries).

The Community was led to opt for taxation at place of destination, which re-established the same tax conditions found at the place
of sale. An additional argument supported this choice, and that was
to prevent each country from succumbing to the temptation to mani-
pulate the tax system to make its producers more competitive abroad.
(It would have been difficult to make the great majority of firms
understand the validity of the theoretical reasoning above, which
flies in the face of their intuition.)

The biggest drawback of this solution is that it necessitates
a border inspection and innumerable formalities in order to apply

---

*Take a hypothetical example: two countries have the same pro-
duction and the same distributed income (equals 100), the same distributions between private and public consumption (70 percent and
30 percent), but different distributions between indirect and direct
taxes (25 percent, 5 percent, and 15 percent, respectively). The
disposable incomes after taxes are 95 and 85, respectively. The
prices of consumer goods, all taxes included, are also 95 and 85.
In order to ensure price parity between countries, we will need:

1. either a rate of exchanged 1/1 with taxes deducted on outgoing goods and reapplied on incoming goods
(sales from A to B 95 - 25 + 15 = 85 or the price in B)
(sales from B to A 85 - 15 + 25 = 95 or the price in A);
2. or taxing at the place of origin, and a rate of exhange such
that the currency unit of A = 85/95 = 0.9 of the currency unit of B.

the system of deducting charges on outgoing goods and reapplying them on incoming goods. This drawback can only be eliminated by the standardization of taxes, not only of VAT rates but of the other indirect taxes. We are still a long way off.

Still, since this is the method opted for, it is psychologically impossible to change in midstream; the only way to get rid of the resulting "tax curtain" at the borders is to set up a standard indirect tax system throughout the EEC with a common definition of added value and to adopt a single rate for all the countries (which does not necessarily mean a uniform rate for all products, provided that the wide range of rates is the same for all countries) and to standardize the other indirect taxes (excise taxes).

On June 29, 1973, the Commission sent new guidelines to the Council that aimed at standardizing the basis of assessment of the VAT and collection methods. However, the text said nothing of the standardization of rates. As for consumption taxes other than the VAT (excise), in March 1972, the Commission presented a proposal to standardize five excise taxes (on mineral oils, tobacco production, hard liquor, beer, and wine) and to gradually eliminate the others. In the first phase, standardization was to be directed at the excise structures, but the Commission recognized that "rate standardization has proved to be very necessary in some respects in order to finally eliminate the compensating measures such as import taxes, export detaxing, inspections, and so on which are currently applied at the border, and which are a great impediment to the unhindered movement of goods."

During 1975, the Commission sent the Council a proposal for bringing the fiscal policies of the Community into line. In the first stage, the planned harmonization would only affect the structure of the tax systems and the bases of taxation; in the second stage, it would affect the income tax rates. The Commission also asked the Council to adopt immediately those proposals concerning the EEC uniform basis of assessment, those concerning harmonization of the excise structures, as well as the proposals on the tax arrangements applying to mergers and on the arrangements applying to parent companies and subsidiaries. Last, it stressed the necessity of setting a fixed period for the gradual harmonization of tax burdens.

Approved by the Council on October 24, 1975, these principles provided the basis of the current discussion on tax harmonization, which concentrate on bringing the structures into line, the problem of the rates themselves having been postponed, although considered essential. In December 1976, a uniform basis of assessment on the VAT was adopted.

Since the beginning, it was thought that the common transport policy might play a major role in influencing the choice of production sites and the exchange of goods.

This is why both the Treaty of Paris and the Treaty of Rome devoted a special chapter to this problem. The great achievement in the European Coal and Steel Community was to eliminate "load-breakings" at the borders by setting up cross-frontier through-rates. This decision was crucial in expanding the movement of coal and goods from the iron and steel industry throughout Community territory. However, for the Common Market itself, no decision of such scope has ever been made.

The two major tests undertaken have been to try to standardize methods of computing cost prices and the ways of setting tariffs. Some real progress has been made, especially in calculating the infrastructure charges, which was the most difficult problem. On the other hand, on the question of tariffs, where viewpoints varied considerably from the outset, hardly any headway has been made. Without necessarily blocking the creation of a real common market, the fact that such disparities persist is certainly one of the reasons for certain very awkward industrial locations, which act against the general interest of Europe.

Other elements come into play that prevent industrial concerns from choosing their sites on the basis of a better use of the factors of production for the entire Community. We might particularly point out those obstacles that still exist to the freedom of establishment for certain professions (especially financial and insurance institutions, for which national markets are as closed off as they were in 1958); the lack of any legal form, a statute, for the European business corporation; and finally, various types of regional aids. In this matter, the objective of correcting social disequilibria, which dominated the picture at the outset, has gradually been supplemented by a desire to secure the best use of the factors of production in the Community as a whole. Both the verdicts on aid given on a national basis and the general Community orientations on the setting up of new plants are increasingly motivated by the wish to channel the location of business so as to strengthen the efficiency of the Community's economy.

The free circulation of capital has gone through several ups and downs, as the first forward steps have been followed by so many steps backward that, as it stands at present, there has been a retrogression. Article 67 of the Treaty was put into effect by two directives in 1960 and 1962, which guaranteed the total liberalization of direct investments and a very advanced liberalization of portfolio investments. These directives did not exclude the possibility of maintaining a certain supervision over exchanges, but in case of a two-tier exchange system, the governments were to keep the financial rate close to the official rate. By enforcing these directives, money controls were abolished in the following years.

But this movement to abolish these restrictions to unhindered capital movements was abruptly brought to a halt by the international monetary crisis of 1968-69. More or less quickly, all the countries, falling back on the Treaty's general safeguard clause, were led to take measures to promote capital movements in certain directions and curtail them in others. Germany and The Netherlands discouraged movements into their countries, while Italy and France (and the United Kingdom) fought against any outflows. The outcome is that, at the present, there are seven officially partitioned markets in the Community of Nine (with Belgium and Luxembourg making up one market, much the same as the United Kingdom and Ireland). However, it must not be forgotten that this de jure situation has been modified by the de facto existence of the Eurodollar market, which is not subject to control and which is a kind of substitute that was spontaneously created to take over the functions formerly filled by the official markets.

Lastly, it is scarcely necessary to point out that no real unified economic area can exist as long as the exchange rates between countries undergo major periodic fluctuations. Firms cannot be asked to act as if they were operating within a single market when they must consider the possibility of—and be on their guard against—changes in exchange rates between member countries. This makes doubly attractive any plans for fixed rates (or a common currency), but it also raises the very real danger that moving so slowly toward a monetary union, or even taking steps backward, can only cause a major setback in the Europeanization of business leaders' ways of thinking. This crucial point will be dealt with again in Chapter 4.

Hence, there are many factors that stand in the way of the completion of a truly unified economic area. Throughout this book, in analyzing foreign trade as well as the structures of production, it must be kept in mind that the changes observed in the last 15 years have taken place in a Community where not all the barriers have been broken down nor all the steps toward harmonization carried out that were foreseen in the Treaty. Thus, in this Community, there remain (potential) factors of evolution that are likely to bring about new changes in the not too distant future.

PRICE EQUALIZATION

One crucial test for a truly unified economic area is the existence of a "single price system" throughout the area. This does not mean that prices of similar products sold under similar conditions (in the same quantities, with the same terms of payment, with the same after sales service, and so forth) are the same everywhere in

the territory but that any disparities result from independent factors
in the behavior of the sellers and buyers, particularly with regard
to transport costs and tax differences.

Such a price system system already exists for most agricultural
produce, since it stems directly from decisions made by the Community
institutions.* It also exists for products of the iron and steel industry,
at least approximately, since the Commission has kept a lookout for
any divergence from Article 60 of the European Coal and Steel Community (ECSC) Treaty (which provided for the publication of price
scales and sales terms by business concerns and which forbids discriminatory practices).

However, there is not enough available information to compare
producers' prices for other goods and services in the various member
countries. Government statistics on prices are few and far between
and are not comparable. At the Community level, standardized
studies are available, but they only cover retail prices.

An analysis of the most recent study to date shows that, depending on the product, the gaps between countries vary greatly,
without there being any clear connection between the size of these
gaps and the kinds of goods. Thus, for goods as different as pork,
whisky, pure wool dress material, rolling vacuum cleaners, and
records, the disparities went no higher than 15 percent in 1970. On
the other hand, they reached or went over 50 percent for goods such
as instant coffee, synthetic blankets, men's cotton shirts, saucepans,
and portable radios.

It would be interesting to know whether these gaps arise in
taxing, distribution, or at the level of the producer himself.

Obviously, differences in tax rates may help create disparities
in the retail prices. Generally speaking, the turnover tax rate is
much higher in France than in the other countries. But the differences

---

* Since 1969, the uniformity of agricultural prices has been
seriously shaken. It was the change in parities (the devaluation of
the French franc, the revaluation of the German mark, and then the
floating exchange rates) that led to the setting-up of the system of
compensatory amounts, intended to protect the farmers from having
their incomes either increase or fall by x percent whenever there
was a devaluation or revaluation of x percent (since agricultural
prices are not fixed in units of account) or to prevent agricultural
transactions from being subjected to the hazards created by the
floating of certain currencies. Nevertheless, this system can also
be thought of as respecting the uniformity of agricultural prices,
but simply using special exchange rates for agricultural produce
that are different from the official exchange rates.

vary considerably from producer to producer. In Table 1.2, four
typical examples are given.

TABLE 1.2

Tax Differences between EEC Countries:
Retail Prices, Tax Inclusive and Tax Exclusive, 1970[a]

(tax rate given in percent)

Product	Germany	France	Italy	Netherlands	Belgium
Meat and meatbased products					
Rate	5.5	7.5	3.3	4	7
Tax inclusive price	118	105	109	111	113
Tax exclusive price	115	100	108	110	109
Radios					
Rate	11	33.3	13.5	12	31
Tax inclusive price	100	138	107	120	119
Tax exclusive price	100	115	105	119	100
Cars (grouping 14 cars for private use)					
Rate	11	33.3	10.5	31.8[b]	18
Tax inclusive price	100	113	101	114	101
Tax exclusive price	106	100	107	101	100
Detergents and scouring powders					
Rate	11	23	7	4	19
Tax inclusive price	114	130	102	139	105
Tax exclusive price	117	120	107	151	100

[a] The enlarging of the Community is too recent a phenomenon
to make it useful to compare the prices between the Six and the three
new members.
[b] Including the special consumer tax.
Source: First report on competition policy, Brussels, 1972.

For meat and meat-based products, the tax rates are not very
different (and, moreover, not very high). Here, the differences
between tax-inclusive prices and untaxed prices are the same. However, the tax rates are very different for radios, and whereas the
tax-inclusive prices range from 100 to 138, the difference ranges
only from 100 to 119 on untaxed prices. In this case, the cheaper
country does not change, whereas the more expensive one does.

For cars, the range is just as narrow, since the ratio of the extremes drops from 114 to 107, with a complete change in the order of the countries. Yet for some consumable household products (such as detergents and scouring powders), tax charges act as a kind of damper, reducing the untaxed price range of 100 to 151 to a tax-inclusive range of 100 to 139. The case is the same for name-brand furniture and refrigerators.

On the whole, taxes account for some of the gaps, but as a total explanation, this factor is very limited. It is rather in the very structures of each market that the answers are likely to be found. The gaps may come from the fact that different prices may be fixed by the producers or, varying from country to country, by the importers. An analysis of the net prices for cars, that is, without taxes and deducting transport and additional costs but including the dealers' profit margin, leads to the following conclusions (around 1970):

1. Most German and Italian manufacturers through their distribution network were putting out their cars at lower net prices, particularly in France and The Netherlands, than on their home markets (with differences ranging from 5 percent to 10 percent).

2. French manufacturers (or their distributers) were selling at higher prices on the markets of other member countries, especially Germany and Italy, than they were on the French market, with the relative differences, according to the model of car, running between 5 percent and usually less than 20 percent.

This large range of prices remains possible due to two factors:

1. On the one hand, a car manufacturer might fix his export price for a certain country according to the price of those cars he wants to compete with, and then consider differences in taste that persist from country to country.

2. On the other hand, this policy has been encouraged by a system that combines exclusive selling rights in a set area with bans on re-export.

If the first factor only reflects a normal diversity throughout the Community, the second falls in with policies that do not totally conform with the Treaty of Rome's Article 85 on competition. The Commission has tried to take action on this, particularly against exclusive distribution agreements and export bans. In particular, exclusive rights agreements act against the setting-up of a single market, since they guarantee the dealer not only the exclusive right to be supplied by the manufacturer but, also, sale distribution rights for concession products in his area. In the Grundig-Consten case, the Commission declared this kind of agreement illegal (a decision supported on all essential points by the Court of Justice's judgment of July 1966), and it has put its energies to bringing about a revamped system, whereby a producer in country A will still be able to grant an exclusive sales franchise to a certain importer in country B, thereby refusing to directly supply any other country B importer, but he will not be able to prohibit his dealers from competing with each other, which will reduce the restrictive scope of exclusive franchises.

The Commission has similarly taken on the task of breaking down the barriers between national markets in several ways: the regulation of export prohibitions built into general sales provisions (the Kodak case, June 1970), clauses intended to keep alive the administrated price system (Agfa-Gevaert case, 1970), and selective distribution systems (Omega case, October 1970). The same objective underlay the Commission's examination (in accordance with Article 86) of the marketing policy of a business in a dominant position (United Brand Company in the banana market) and led it to prohibit any action by this firm to partition the market.

Obviously, these efforts can only gradually bear fruit. Also, it must be added that it was only around 1970 that the Commission, strengthened by its ground-breaking decision, started active intervention by prohibiting certain actions or by calling firms to account. It is clear that it will still take some time to come close to a total uniformity of untaxed prices throughout the EEC (at least the Community of Six; spreading this to the three new members will require additional time).

Lastly, information coming from business corporations gives the very clear impression that, for many products, producers still regard the Community as far from unified. This is the case, not only because of technical or tax regulations but also because of the buyers' behavior, especially if a private consumer or an administration. Therein lies a major difference between the European market and the American market—that is, the existence or not of a unified market (even if noticeable differences of taste do exist between the East and West coasts of the United States, it is still a unified market). This diversity may well persist, continuing to be one of Europe's peculiar characteristics and cultural assets.

THE RAPID GROWTH IN
INTRA-COMMUNITY TRADE AND SPECIALIZATION

The second test for a unified economic area is increased internal trade and the specialization phenomenon.*

The amount of intra-Community trade has increased far more rapidly than world trade (the growth rates at current prices were 15 percent and 8 percent per annum, respectively, between 1959 and 1971). Likewise, in each member country, intra-Community trade has increased faster than trade with countries outside the Community. Between the Six, trade has increased sixfold and trade with outside countries threefold. This means that intra-Community trade currently accounts for one-half the Community total, as opposed to a little more than one-quarter 25 years ago and 30 percent in 1958.

It is true that trade between the Six was already increasing faster than trade with the rest of the world in pre-Community times: between 1951 and 1958, the multiplying factors were 1.9 and 1.6, respectively. Nevertheless, it is undeniable that opening the borders provided a real stimulus to exchanges between Common Market partners. But the effects of this stimulus only became apparent gradually. Apart from the observed growth of 1959, which compensated for the low economic activity in 1958, it was not until 1962 that there was a growth in intra-Community trade markedly greater than that with outside countries. In retrospect, it seems that it was necessary to reach a certain stage in customs "disarmament," as well as in the dismantling of all quota systems (and probably the setting-up of trade networks as well), before internal trade could really make strides.

Since 1967, the rapid growth of intra-Community trade has continued its even advance, but it has been accompanied as well by a noticeable pickup in trade with external countries. The compared elasticities of intra-Community trade in relation to external trade explain this development very well: 1.5 during 1951-58, 2.6 between 1958 and 1967, and 1.7 between 1967 and 1971.

Although this growth rate has been high everywhere, it has not been equal in all the countries. One is immediately struck by the great increase in French and Italian imports, as well as in Italian

---

*In this section of the book, we have preferred to deal only with the Community of Six, where the phenomena of specialization have had the time to emerge. As for the three new partners, it is still too early to discuss their case, given the unsettling effect of the current slump conditions.

TABLE 1.3

Trade Evolution, by Member Countries, EEC, and World, 1959–70
(multiplying factor 70/59)

Exports	Imports						
	Germany	France	Italy	Netherlands	Benelux Countries	EEC	World
Germany	—	5.7	6.4	4.5	4.7	5.2	3.5
France	4.9	—	7.7	7.1	4.5	5.4	3.2
Italy	5.7	9.9	—	8.2	5.3	6.8	4.6
Netherlands	4.9	6.4	7.0	—	3.1	4.5	3.3
BLEU*	6.7	8.0	7.4	3.1	—	5.2	3.5
EEC	5.4	7.0	6.9	4.3	4.1	—	3.5
World	3.5	3.7	4.5	3.4	3.3	3.6	—

* Belgo–Luxemburgan Economic Union
Source: SOEC

TABLE 1.4

Comparison of Foreign Trade of Member Countries, 1970*

Country of Origin	Imports			Exports		
	In Billions of Dollars	Percentage of GNP	Dollars per Person	In Millions of Dollars	Percentage of GNP	Dollars per Person
Germany	29.8	16	480	34.2	18	550
France	18.9	13	370	17.7	12	350
Italy	14.9	16	270	13.2	14	240
Netherlands	13.4	43	1,020	11.8	38	900
BLEU	11.3	43	1,130	11.6	44	1,160
EEC	88.4	18	460	88.5	18	460

* Goods only.
Source: SOEC

exports. In contrast, the Benelux countries' growth rate for trade
has been far lower, particularly in imports. Germany falls between
the two extremes. (See Table 1.3.)

The growth in intra-Community imports has been all the greater
where the national industry was highly protected and, equally, where
the relation of foreign trade to GNP was the lowest. (See Table 1.4.)
Indeed, there is a certain threshold where further opening toward the
outside becomes difficult.

The rate of annual growth in intra-Community trade varied
greatly from one branch to another, ranging between 7 percent and
22 percent (see Table 1.5). Moreover, the top-rated branches are
not necessarily the ones where the Community's internal demand is
highest: for instance, the high growth rate in the clothing and furniture

TABLE 1.5

Rate of Growth in Intra-Community
Trade, by Industry, 1958-70

	Yearly Growth Rate in Percent	Elasticity of Intra-Community Trade in Relation to European and American Countries with Developed Market Economies
Clothing	22.4	1.6
Wood and furniture	20.9	2.7
Transport equipment	20.2	1.8
Rubber	18.3	1.4
Paper, cardboard	18.1	2.1
Leather and shoes	17.8	1.1
Chemicals	17.6	1.5
Electrical machinery	17.2	1.1
Metal goods	16.9	1.5
Nonelectrical machinery	16.5	1.4
Building materials, glass, and so forth	15.1	1.4
Press and publishing	13.9	1.2
Agriculture and foodstuffs	13.6	2.5
Fats	13.3	—
Textiles	12.2	1.0
Iron and steel	11.9	1.3
Raw materials, except textiles	10.1	4.0
Mineral fuels	7.2	2.3

Source: Compiled by the author.

industries reflects a greater variety available to consumers. A comparison of the elasticity of intra-Community trade with trade in an area with similar economic structures, and grouping together the Community (exclusive of intra-Community trade), the European Free Trade Association (EFTA), and North America, shows that, except for textiles, intra-Community trade has expanded in all branches at a faster rate than external trade.

Over the last few years, various commentators thought it possible to assess the effectiveness of European construction by looking at the development of intra-Community trade, and they drew rather optimistic conclusions from the rapidity of its development. This approach is too simplistic: international trade is not a goal in itself but only a means to attain certain objectives, mainly an increase in the efficiency of production and a wider range of goods available to consumers.

A growth in trade can only be regarded as worthwhile insofar as it makes it possible to reach these goals. This is the case when the intensification of trade results from more advanced specialization by the producers, whether justified by geographic considerations (at ground level or below ground) or by economies of scale or whether, without any physical reason or regardless of size, it occurs in businesses that are highly efficient due to their management. (As seen later, it seems that a large proportion of intra-Community trade belongs to this kind of specialization.)

On the other hand, certain exchanges are made possible when certain producers, taking advantage of dominant positions, aggressively conquer foreign markets, albeit often temporarily, by undercutting prices or, even, going as far as dumping. Finally, opening borders may set off flows of goods simply because of bad information on the prices and the compared qualities of the products from several possible suppliers. In any case, the increase in trade does not mean an increase in efficiency. Moreover, the treaties provide for Community intervention to prevent such cases, either through its rules on competition (Articles 85 and 86 of the Treaty of Rome), its restrictions on dumping (Article 91 of the Treaty of Rome) and, in the case of the coal and steel, its required publication of price lists (Article 60 of the Treaty of Paris).

Thus, it is seen that the volume of intra-Community trade cannot, in itself, be a satisfactory yardstick to measure the success of the Common Market. Only in trying to find out what this increase in foreign trade means can its usefulness to the Community be assessed.

In the following pages, it is hoped that some light will be thrown on the subject by studying the phenomena of specialization between countries. (A clearer picture should appear in the following chapter on the development of production structures.)

If the specialization of trade in one country for certain goods is to be accurately measured, the selection of one product as the indicator will not work. This product's share in the country's total exports will give an incomplete picture if it is not compared with the similar figure of other countries. One country's share in the trade of one product must also be compared with this country's share in the total trade.

Therefore, to compare the specialization of various countries in intra-Community trade, we are led to use a complicated indicator, simultaneously taking into account the exports of a product and total exports, for the country under consideration, as well as for all countries, as expressed in the formula:

$$k = \frac{X^r_i}{X^r} : \frac{X^i}{X}$$

with X^r_i = intra-EEC exports from country i for the industrial branch r;

X^r = intra-EEC exports of all member countries for branch r;

Xi = total intra-EEC exports from country i; and

X = total intra-EEC exports of all member countries.

We will call this indicator the coefficient of predominance.[*]

Contrary to what might be expected, an overall look at 19 branches of industry shows less concentration of trade per country in 1970 than in 1958 and 1955.[†] (See Table 1.6)

This cutback in trade concentration comes out of two movements. First, the relative intensity of certain countries' predominance in some industrial branches has fallen off—this is the case of Western Germany in metal working and electrical and mechanical engineering,

---

[*] When the coefficient has a value of one, this means that the product r's share in the total exports is the same for country i and for all the EEC ($\frac{X^r_i}{X_i} = \frac{X^r}{X}$), or that the country i's share in Community exports is the same for product r and for exports as a whole ($\frac{X^r_i}{X^r} = \frac{X_i}{X}$): product r is an "average" product as far as the exports of country i go. If the coefficient value is over one, we can say that product r is predominant (a leading product) among country i's exports. This idea of predominance is relative, that is, in relation to the average Community situation.

[†] In Chapter 5, it will be seen that this holds less true for exports to the Third World.

TABLE 1.6

Coefficients of Predominance in Intra-EEC Trade, 1970

Industry	Germany*	France	Italy	Netherlands	Belgium, Luxembourg
Machinery, except electric machines	++	-	+	--	--
Electrical machinery	+	=	+	--	-
Metal goods	+	-	=	--	=
Transport equipment	+	+	=	--	=
Chemicals	=	=	-	+	--
Mineral fuels	=	--	=	++	--
Wood and furniture	=	-	+	-	+
Building materials, glass and so forth	=	-	+	--	+
Iron and steel	=	=	--	--	++
Paper, cardboard	=	-	--	++	+
Fats	=	-	--	++	-
Rubber	-	++	=	=	=
Press and publishing	-	-	++	-	=
Nonferrous metals	-	-	--	-	++
Raw materials, except for mineral fuels (other than textile fibers)	-	++	--	++	-
Textiles	-	=	=	=	+
Clothing	--	-	++	-	=
Leather and shoes	--	=	++	--	-
Agriculture and foodstuffs	--	++	=	++	-

++ stands for very high level of specialization; coefficient of predominance >1.5.

+ stands for rather high level of specialization; coefficient of predominance >1.1 and <1.5.

= stands for average specialization; coefficient of predominance >0.9 and <1.1.

- stands for low level of specialization; coefficient of predominance >0.5 and <0.9.

-- stands for very low level of specialization; coefficient of predominance <0.5.

* For Germany, the industrial branches are ranked in descending order of the coefficient of predominance (in 1970).

Germany handles the greatest share of intra-Community trade (32 percent).

Source: Compiled by the author.

two industries that are, by tradition, representative of German industry. Though Germany's position was strong in 1970, it was on the decline in relation with its 1955 position. Second, the relative weakness of concentration of other countries in these branches is tending to diminish—this is the case in France for the same branches where the country's industrialization effort is making itself felt.

However, if we apply the same coefficient of predominance at a much more detailed level on far more similar goods, singling out several hundreds of articles under a number of headings, we arrive at results that vary greatly and find that very marked phenomena of specialization persist. One is struck by the fact that for almost every article, there are one or two countries that are highly specialized, with other countries lagging far behind in intra-Community trade for these articles.[2]

TABLE 1.7

Coefficients of Predominance
for Nonelectrical Machinery of EEC Countries, 1969
(numbers of products)

Country of Origin	More than 2	Between 2 and 1.5	Between 1.5 and 1.1	Between 1.1 and 0.9	Between 0.9 and 0.5	Less than 0.5
Germany	10	14	7	5	5	—
France	5	1	4	5	12	14
Italy	11	7	6	—	—	10
Netherlands	1	—	—	2	3	35
Belgium	—	1	2	1	5	32

Source: Compiled by the author.

These two facts may be illustrated by the group of nonelectrical machines shown in Table 1.7.

For the whole group, the coefficients of predominance range, depending on the countries, between 1.6 and 0.5. Yet, for each of the 41 products in this group, the highest coefficient of predominance never drops below 1.6 (except for forklift trucks), and it is over 2 for 23 products, or more than half. At the same time, the smallest coefficients go very low; for 75 percent of the products, one country at least is practically eliminated as an exporter in the Common Market. France offers an excellent example of the phenomenon of specialization: on the whole, France exports relatively less than its competitors (coefficient 0.8); but the coefficient goes over 2 for 5 products and 1.1 for 10 others, whereas it drops to 0.5 for 14 products.

Comparing countries brings interesting differences to light. Thus, we see that in Germany and Italy, the number of high-predominance products is the same, but whereas this is true for all of Germany's products, Italy's position is weak for 25 percent of her products. Germany's long industrial tradition gives her a larger foothold, while Italy's younger mechanical engineering industry holds few positions, but holds them with particular intensity. For France, specialization is clearly less marked.

Finally, a more detailed approach can be taken for two product categories where the growth rate in intra-Community trade has been particularly high and whose production structures will be analyzed in the next chapter, namely, car manufacturing and household appliances.

The high tariff barriers for cars in 1958 protected the Italian and French markets (a rate of 40 percent to 45 percent for the former and 30 percent for the latter) much more than the German market (with a rate of approximately 13 percent). Added to this were the quantitative restrictions in France and Belgium, the unfavorable import procedures, and, finally, the technical hindrances, such as government car security standards.

Under these conditions, the share of total imports in supplying the major producing countries' markets was small—8 percent in Germany, 2 percent in France and Italy, and 14 percent in Belgium.[*]

On the other hand, in The Netherlands, where national production played a rather small part, imports met 85 percent of the needs.

On January 1, 1961, the quantitative restrictions between member countries were abolished. In the middle of 1968, the last of a series of tariff cuts ended the intra-Community customs barriers, which had already been reduced by 50 percent by 1962-63.

Between 1958 and 1970, there was a great increase in the part played by other member countries in the supplying of each country's market. This percentage rose to more than 28 percent in Italy in 1970, as opposed to 2 percent in 1958; to almost 25 percent in West Germany in 1970 (7 percent in 1958); 16 percent in France in 1970 (1 percent in 1958); and 49 percent in the BLEU in 1970 (14 percent in 1958). (In The Netherlands, the 1970 share was only slightly higher than the already high level of 1958). Moreover, there seems

---

[*] This is not counting components (imported) to be assembled on site.

to have been a sharp increase in the share of imports over the last few years, particularly in France and Italy.

It seems that, coupled with the elimination of tariffs, the abolition of quantitative restrictions has played a major part in the growth of trade. This would explain to a large degree the dramatic increase in the share of imports from France (from 1 percent to 9 percent), from Italy (from 2 percent to 15 percent), and from Belgium (from 11 percent to 23 percent) between 1958 and 1963, that is, in the period when customs duties were only cut by half. In Germany, where there were no quantitative restrictions, the rise was insignificant.

In the household appliance sector, the setting-up of the Common Market provided a real stimulus to intra-Community trade: between 1960 and 1970, at constant prices, there was a sixfold increase (all the more dramatic, as there is a tendency toward current price stability and, therefore, toward a drop in "real" prices). (See Table 1. 8.)

TABLE 1.8

Evolution of Intra-Community Trade in
Household Electrical Appliances, 1960, 1965, and 1970
(millions of units of account)

Appliances	1960	1965	1970
Refrigerators	28.2	74.5	108.2
Washing machines	12.7	64.5	138.6
Small appliances	13.8	22.8	146.6
TV sets	29.6	51.9	143.2
Radios	29.4	51.2	113.6

Note: Until 1971, the unit of account equaled $1. Since then, it has been defined as a weighted average of currency of the member countries and, in 1976, was made equal to about $1.20.

Source: SOEC

For refrigerators and washing machines, the highest rate of growth in trade was recorded between 1960 and 1965 (reaching more than 400 percent for washing machines). In television sets, the growth rate was higher between 1965 and 1970, reaching 340 percent and thus surpassing the growth rate of the other appliances.

The customs duties, which more or less protected the different national product before the advent of the Common Market, had apparently been the main obstacle to trade.

In Italy, which had the highest customs duties in the Common Market, one might have expected the imports from the EEC to rise greatly as the customs union progressively came into effect. This forecast has not been fulfilled (except in vacuum cleaners), and in fact, Italian industry has become a great exporter. In France, imports from EEC members reached very high levels in the years immediately following the abolition of quotas, the last having been eliminated in 1961. This shows that customs duties were not the only factor; other factors came into play as well, especially the elimination of import quotas and, above all, the awareness that additional effort was necessary to make the national productions more competitive.

The case of Italian-made washing machines provides a very telling example—the breaking into foreign markets by the Italians was backed up by quite different and aggressive marketing techniques. These two products rank highest on the list of the most dramatic examples of market transformations and of the rise of one country to the rank of a top exporter: in five years, Italy's share rose from 5 percent to 43 percent for internal trade in washing machines—during the same time, the price had undergone a fivefold increase. (See Table 1.9.)

Yet, as will be seen in the following chapter, Italian corporations have turned to mass production, which has brought in its wake economies of scale, thus making the prices of their electrical appliances competitive and setting off the boom in exports.

These observations drawn from foreign trade statistics support the impressions given by the few available production statistics, and from these data, a working hypothesis may be put forward.

The narrowing of the gap (in terms of the coefficient of predominance) between one country and another in relation to the 19 industrial branches may be due to the fact that, in 1970, none of the countries was really unrepresented in any branch, or, inversely, no country really stood by itself in any of them. At the root of this phenomenon lie the industrialization campaigns in France and Italy and the increased drawing together of the macroeconomic structures of the EEC countries in general.

On the other hand, the considerable disparities noted in specific products in any particular branch suggest that the countries that were lagging behind in the first instance have succeeded in finding and filling a number of gaps which were either unfilled or which were easily approachable through lack of competitive resistance. The repetition of this phenomenon in each industrial branch might thus explain that there is a reduction in the general disparities for the branch as a whole.

This would confirm the often expressed idea that, apart from a few products, there are no physical factors at play that favor locating

TABLE 1.9

Household Electrical Appliances: Domestic Demand and Intra–Community Trade—Germany, France, and Italy, 1960, 1965, and 1970

Country of Origin	Refrigerators			Washing Machines		
	1960	1965	1970	1960	1965	1970
Domestic Demand Covered by National Supply						
Germany	97	89	67	96	93	80
France	98	76	41	97	91	79
Italy	94	98	98	85	97	—
The Different Countries' Share in Intra–Community Trade						
Germany	48	25	12	63	42	30
France	13	7	2	20	12	13
Italy	37	68	84	5	43	56

Source: SOEC trade statistics.

24

production units for a product in one region over another. Rather, it is the legacy of history, coupled with the drive of present-day business leaders, which secures a predominant position for a country at any given time in the production and export of certain goods. These positions are consequently much less stable than if they were the result of objective factors, and changes are, thus, all the more rapid.

It is necessary to draw attention to the fact that, apart from the chemical industry in The Netherlands, most of these striking phenomena took place in the beginning days of the Common Market and leveled off after 1965. In other words, by 1965, the major development trends were set. This suggests that the abolition of restrictions and quotas (in 1961) played a major role. Moreover, one should not overlook the possible actions of the entrepreneurs, who may have foreseen the coming competition and acted quickly before its effects were felt, leaving themselves in a strong position on the market from which they could outstrip their competitors.

Without any doubt, the Common Market of goods has become a striking reality. Regardless of the few remaining obstacles, the free movement of goods now exists for goods subject to private buying. It is far from being the same case for public tenders. Differing in this from the national governments, industrial and business concerns have to a large extent, and very quickly, played the Common Market game. They started as soon as the quantitative restrictions were eliminated. Building up trade networks and putting active trade practices into work set off a dramatic boom in intra-Community trade, which was very often linked with a continued or strengthened specialization.

Yet, there is still a rather long way to go to attain a truly integrated economic area. Above all, it is the different tax systems that make necessary the customs barriers, which bring about the "coexistence" of national economies and encourage price disparities throughout the Community territory.

NOTES

1. See Rapport sur les problèmes posés par les taxes sur le chiffre d'affaires dans le Marché Commun (called Rapport Tinberger) (Luxembourg: European Coal and Steel Community (ECSC), 1953).

2. The fact that various writers on the Common Market, working from sets of headings that were too aggregated, that is, too few in numbers, came too rapidly to the conclusion that the Common Market had reduced specialization between countries makes it necessary to take a very detailed approach. For an example, refer to Mayor and

Hays, Another Look at the Common Market (National Institute
Economic Review, London, November 1970). This study broke down
industries under 28 headings.

2

DEVELOPMENT OF
PRODUCTION STRUCTURES

In many branches of industry, industrial production is currently characterized by dropping costs as a function of increased production. These phenomena of increasing returns to scale come into play whether constructing production units or dealing with the length of production runs. This is one of the major present-day characteristics of industry, far more pronounced today than 30 or 40 years ago, and which can be observed as well in certain so-called tertiary activities, such as banking and insurance.

This basic concept of economies of scale needs to be completed by a "concept of minimal threshold": not only does the unit cost decrease as the output increases but, for technical and financial reasons, the size of the factory or concern must go over a certain threshold.[1]

In order to profit fully from the economies of scale, a sufficient market is needed, not only to permit the firm to reach its optimum production capacity but also to bring into play a certain number of production units on the same market, thereby stimulating a certain competition, which is crucial if businesses are to be dynamic and if the introduction of innovations is to be speeded up. As it is, the markets of each European country (even medium-sized countries, such as Germany, France, or Great Britain) are, in fact, insufficient in many branches of industry to provide outlets for two or three firms of optimum size. This is the origin of the idea of a big market that would promote specialization between firms and make it possible for each to reach a production level where the cost would be near the minimum, while maintaining sufficient competition at the same time.

Four actors, or groups of actors, have taken part in the reorganization of production structures throughout Community territory. These are Community firms, foreign firms, national governments, and Community institutions.

The changes we have observed for more than 15 years result from the combined strategies of these four groups. In some cases, the strategies have operated independently; in some cases, they have been coordinated; and in some cases, they have been opposed to one another.

In the following section, we will begin by clarifying the part played by the various actors and then proceed to describe the types of reorganizations of industrial structures, illustrated by a few specific representative cases (such as household electrical goods, the car industry, and data processing). Energy and agriculture will be discussed in a later section, along with research policy, because drawing up a common policy has been attempted for these three fields.

STRATEGIES OF THE ACTORS

Growth in Community Intervention

Side by side with the gradual elimination of obstacles to the movement of goods and the factors of production, there are more active interventions which aim at curtailing certain developments.

For this purpose, the Commission has three very important instruments available: Article 86 of the EEC Treaty, the overseeing of national aids and subsidies, and directive documents. To these could also be added Community financial intervention.

These instruments have been brought into use only very recently or only very sparingly.

The course of action followed by the Commission regarding concentrations is laid out in Article 86. Contrary to what happens in certain countries (in Germany, for example, as well as in coal and steel industries under the provisions of the ECSC Treaty), for mergers and concentrations, there is no investigation or authorization beforehand. Any investigation or supervision comes after the fact, since Article 86 prohibits "any abuse of a dominant position within the Common Market or in a substantial part of it." The Commission's first interventions based on this Article were made during 1971 (the GEMA case, Gesellschaft für Musikalische Aufführungs–und mechanische Verviel–fältigungsrechte, and the Continental Can case).

---

* These two decisions show the Commission's wish to deal simultaneously with the two ways Article 86 might be applied: that is, determination of abusive behavior on the market and, also, a restriction of the consumer's free choice by concentrations, whereby a firm

Thus, for more than 10 years, Article 86 was able to influence the concentration movement (mostly by the way firms thought the Commission might apply it). On the other hand, for the last several years, the Commission has increased the number of its decisions, striving particularly to curtail the diversified sales policies in the different Community areas. It furthermore asked the Council to adapt a regulation on the supervision of concentrations that would make it possible for the Commission to step in more quickly and more effectively.

As for the directive documents concerning sectoral structures, a special place must be given to the general objectives of the ECSC (which for over a decade has been restricting itself to the general objectives for the steel industry) and to the guidelines laid down by Euratom (European Community for Atomic Energy).

On the other hand, the general Treaty of Rome does not bring up the question of the structures of production and, thus, does not provide for any specific action, except for agriculture and transport (that is, less than 15 percent of the GNP 15 years ago and less than 10 percent today). The Treaty's silence on this problem explains why the Community institutions began to be concerned about this problem at a rather late date. Actually, for some time, the Commission took the view that competition was the instrument necessary to promote change in production structures and that the major course of action should be that this competition be maintained by keeping a close watch on agreements between firms and on mergers and by making sure that government aids and subsidies did not interfere with the smooth working of the market. However, pushed by events, the Commission has gradually been led to intervene in certain industries.

The first official document where the necessity of direct action on production structures was made explicit is the second Medium-Term Economic Policy Program, essentially worked out during 1967 and adopted by the Commission on May 12, 1967. Noting that "dynamic economies are characterized by a constant transformation of the structures of demand and production," this document concludes that "it is especially desirable that Member States and Community Institutions share their views on this problem," and goes further by setting

---

in a dominating position practically eliminates competition by taking over a competitor. In accord with the general objectives of the EEC Treaty, Commission intervention aims at preventing firms in a dominant position from hindering the setting-up of a system to protect against a distortion of competition in the Common Market or from undermining the continued existence of such competition (Commission of the European Communities, First Report on Competition Policy [April 1972], p. 74).

forth the problems of the electronics and shipbuilding sectors,
suggesting some desirable directions to take.[2]

The second important document is the Commission's March
1970 memorandum to the Council on the Community's industrial
policy. It stresses the fact that 12 years after the founding of the
Community,

> working out a common industrial development policy to
> promote the creation of what might be called a European
> industrial fabric has proved to be essential in order to
> simultaneously ensure the irreversible foundations of the
> economic unity, and soon, the political unity of Western
> Europe, the pursuit of economic growth and a reasonable
> degree of technological autonomy vis à vis our big non-
> European partners.

Yet this document remains very general, since it is written that
"the object of the present Memorandum is not to analyze the different
sectoral problems nor to propose particular solutions for this or that
industrial sector." Thus, it is only in these subsequent texts that
specific proposals concerning certain sectors of activity are put
forward. Attention should particularly be drawn to texts on textile
industries, the aircraft industry, and electrical engineering, all
three of which came out in 1971, as well as to a document on the paper
pulp industry in 1974.

Except for coal and steel and, to a certain extent, the nuclear
industry, as well as shipbuilding—the problems of these industries
were tackled because of the concern to bring the national subsidies
into line—it was not until 1970 that definite positions were taken
regarding some industrial sectors.

Government aids and subsidies to firms are a very effective
means of bringing about a reorganization of production structures,
and they are widespread throughout industrialized countries. This is
why the Treaty of Rome explicitly dealt with this problem. First, the
first paragraph of Article 92 states that government aids favoring
certain firms or the production of certain goods and which affect trade
by distorting or threatening to distort competition are incompatible
with the Common Market. Second (in the second and third paragraphs),
it lists certain categories of aids, rather broadly defined, which are,
or may be considered as, compatible.

Community control of national aids is necessary for two main
reasons:

1. to prevent those aids that are not essential from indirectly
calling back into question the customs union and the equality of

opportunity which must exist between the Community's economic agents—also to ensure that the best allocation of the factors of production is carried out and to avoid putting these factors of production to use on things that yield little profit;

2. to permit aids in those situations where, under suitable conditions, the play of the market alone does not make it possible to attain certain social or economic ends.

It is along these general lines that the Commission's course of action has developed, both for regional and sectoral aids.

Regional aids, when adequate, can provide an essential instrument for balanced regional development, which is one of the Treaty's objectives. However, they led the member states to outbid each other to attract investors. By making the efforts undertaken more costly and preventing the backward areas from profiting from the necessary priorities, these bids were compromising the looked-for balance.

After several years' work carried on in collaboration with the member states, the Commission decided to apply some basic principles to these aids calculated to ward off their harmful effects.[3]

The solution of coordination adopted, which did not apply to the Community's central regions where the effects of the outbidding were the most worrisome, for the most part meant setting a ceiling on regional aids of 20 percent of investments, expressed in "net subsidy equivalent" (after taxing). Not only was this solution supposed to make regional aids more proportional to the seriousness of the difficulties, but setting a limit to the aids for central regions was also supposed to increase the effectiveness of those efforts in favor of so-called peripheral regions, where the problems are the most serious.

In 1975, the Commission decreed new principles to be applied over a period of three years (and which are currently in force for the enlarged Community as a whole) that expanded principles which had been previously laid down. The "transparence" of aids is undergoing extensive research, and different intensity limits have been set out; the Community territory has been divided into four categories, according to their respective stages of development and their special problems. For the first category, the limits have been frozen at the maximum level already reached: they often exceed 35 percent. For the other categories, they have been set at 30 percent, 25 percent, and 20 percent, respectively.

At the current stage of development of the Common Market, the granting of sectoral subsidies, whether for transforming basic industries or for boosting advanced technology industries, may be justified by the difficulties often found at the Community level, or at least in several member states. In these kind of cases, the Community strives to avoid simply "reacting" to the uncoordinated initiatives taken by national governments, which, because of certain "escalations," would lose their effectiveness while undermining the common interest.

On the basis of a diagnosis of any given sector's development, the Commission can take the first steps by determining a "Community framework" in which foreseeable government actions should fall and which would include the industrial objectives to be reached, as well as a description of the means it would prefer to have used.

It was on this basis that the Commission took steps to establish limits for subsidies in the textile sector (July 1971) and the aircraft sector (July 1972). In other branches, the situation was the same from one member state to the next, and this made it possible to directly introduce a Community system concerning aids: this was the case when, on July 28, 1969, the Council adopted the set of guidelines concerning the quantity of aids to the shipbuilding industry and which, in setting the ceiling for aids at 10 percent of the selling price of ships, had as its aim to correct distorted competition on the international market.

A later proposal, adopted in July 1972, set a lower and sliding ceiling (5 percent in 1972, 4 percent in 1973, and 3 percent in 1974), while broadening the idea of aids. Yet another proposal was adopted in July 1975 on the principle of eliminating aids to shipbuilding as of December 3, 1975, except for a few temporary exceptions.

Finally, besides these overall actions, the Commission was led to give its decisions case by case regarding sectoral aids set up by the member states. Those industries particularly concerned with these aids are data processing, the paper and paper pulp industry, cinematography, Italian sulphur production, and the iron and steel industry.

The length of time necessary to actually implement Article 92 becomes more understandable if one considers the very ambiguity of the idea of "aid." Furthermore, the situation of each country may vary greatly, as well as each country's conception of intervention for regional or sectoral ends. Finally, one must take into consideration the unwillingness of governments to have their freedom to intervene limited in those areas where they have to cope with problems of a social nature, or in those sectors that are wrongly or rightly considered disadvantaged in international competition, or lastly, in those industries considered basic to national independence.

One might consider the possibility of the granting of aid being subject to Community decision and financed by the Community budget. Until now, except for agriculture and the "common undertaking" defined by the Euratom Treaty, no such procedure has been applied, but the Commission proposed something of this kind with its project for industrial development contracts.

In short, the Community has taken its positions too recently for these proposals to have had any major effect on production structures, and the statistical information at hand reveals an autonomous movement but slightly influenced by any precise Community interventions. Yet the series of initiatives taken in the last three or four years, whether concerning competition policy or industrial policy, will probably have profound effects in the future.

It must be added that, although the Treaty (particularly in Articles 99, 100, and 101) called for national laws and forms of taxation to be harmonized, progress has been slow, and success is a long way off. Thus, up to now, the development of industrial structures has taken place in circumstances where legislations, administrative regulations, and taxation have been far off the goals set up by the Treaty of Rome. The context of these years of development has been one in which national disparities have remained disparities that can, in some cases, seriously curtail economically justified transformations.

National Governments

Entry into the Common Market in 1958 was very much a leap in the dark, and several of the governments of member countries sought to put the firms in their own countries in as good a position as possible to withstand foreign competition. They did this by having recourse to methods that were not forbidden by the Treaty of Rome (such as fiscal attitudes to self-financing, the extension of regional aids, infrastructure development, education and training, and, in some countries, influence on undertakings in the public sector).

The approaches to these problems are extremely different from one country to another; yet, there is some tendency for these approaches to draw closer together. France has long been the country with the most state intervention—at least in proclamations. The drawing up of government Five Year Plans provided an opportunity to reflect on the development desired for industrial structures and paved the way for certain public interventions. More recently, the French government has exercised a control over takeovers of French firms by foreign corporations and this has provided it with many opportunities to redirect, or to try to redirect, some reorganizations of production structures. In the United Kingdom, the government has also actively intervened in industrial reorganization, through the Industrial Reorganisation Corporation, particularly by promoting mergers and specializations. Germany, on the contrary, especially during the Ehrard era, placed its trust in competition mechanisms and the controls of the Bundeskartellamt (the Antitrust Office) to lead to optimum structures. However, in the last few years, there have been cases of government intervention, particularly in those industries that are the most technologically advanced. In Italy, the government's strategy is based mainly on its wish to reduce the gap between the north and south of Italy and has found its main instrument of action in the public sector. Lastly, in The Netherlands, the official doctrine stands strictly opposed to all forms of specific state intervention in business decisions.

Behavior of Community Firms

Among Community firms, four main lines of behavior may be noted:

1. No change in previous lines of behavior: This does not signify an absence of development or innovation among these firms but rather that the opening of the frontiers did not have any noteworthy effect on their current management or on their investment decisions. This position was to be seen among a considerable number of firms catering to local markets, which, before 1958, were scarcely affected by competition over the whole of their national territory (especially in the bigger countries) and which, therefore, felt no alarm about foreign competition and had no particular desire to conquer foreign markets. The building industry is a good example of this type of behavior.

2. Defensive reaction: The essential objective in such cases is to keep approximately the same share of the market (usually, the national market) as before. Two tactical approaches were noted. On the one hand, the firm might seek to cope with foreign competition by reducing its production costs, either by investment for modernization or by some degree of specialization. The other defensive approach consisted in operating through cartels and similar agreements it is difficult to say how great a use was made of this, but there can be no doubt that it was indeed used.

3. Offensive action inside the Community: In these cases, the firm concerned sought to use the opening of borders to conquer the new external markets. This behavior is of special interest in those industries in which economies of scale could play an important part. In such cases, the conquest of external markets not only makes it possible to enlarge the firm's commercial outlets but also tends to reduce unit costs and so enable it to preserve or extend its share of the internal market.

4. Offensive action at world level: In this case, the firm sought to take advantage of the economies of scale in a wider market and find itself a place in the world market. It tended to regard the

Community market as unduly limited, and its strategy developed immediately, either at the European level or at the world level. A strategy on these lines may be carried out by the firm on its own initiative or with the help of its government. The former was the case with various multinational firms that, even before 1958, were accustomed to thinking internationally and were just as interested in development in nonmember countries as in Community territory, which they considered to be unduly small. This goes some way toward explaining the fact that it was only to a moderate extent that such firms sought to establish themselves on the markets of other member countries, whether by merging with, or by buying up, smaller firms. The second case applies to larger firms that work in fields where the risk is great or where aid from public sources is considered a necessity before new operations can be undertaken. The clearest instance is that of the aircraft industry, in which a number of big European firms agreed among themselves to launch cooperative projects, such as the Concorde and the Airbus, with financial backing on a massive scale from the public authorities.

Foreign Firms

Foreign firms in this context means American firms, European firms from countries outside the Common Market (especially, Swiss and Swedish firms), and, more recently, Japanese firms. They too, might have reacted either defensively or offensively. Their defensive attitude was aimed at neutralizing the possible adverse effects on their business of the elimination of barriers in the Community. Their offensive attitude, on the other hand, was aimed at deliberately profiting from the big unified market that was being set up.

There were three basic approaches, all of which could be applied both offensively and defensively:

1. Expansion of existing subsidiaries: Outstanding examples of this occurred in the car-manufacturing and data-processing industries.

2. The setting-up of new subsidiaries where none previously existed: This case was the least frequent.

3. The takeover of existing firms: This was done in order to make use of existing production facilities (for example, the Chrysler takeover of Simca), or of high-quality research groups (takeover of Bull by General Electric), or—and this occurred most often—in order to secure quick command of a marketing organization that was thoroughly familiar with the peculiarities of each of the European national markets.

TYPOLOGY OF REORGANIZATIONS

Two major changes are to be expected from these various strategies on the part of firms and public authorities: specialization between countries (described in the previous chapter) and a concentration of productions units.

Taking the latter, from the available information, which is very incomplete or incommensurable,[4] a very clear picture emerges: "From 1962 to 1969 a wave of industrial combinations took place which hit almost all countries and industries, and which increasingly intensified."[5]

This reorganization of production structures was mostly carried out between firms of an individual country. Yet the number of international operations was on the rise: from 1,350 in 1966, it rose to 2,158 in 1971 (by comparison, the total number of mergers in France in 1968 was on the order of 2,240). If the majority of these international operations were limited to setting up simple subsidiaries, around 40 percent were of a more complex nature—setting up joint subsidiaries or buying in—which usually involved two firms, but, in approximately one out of every seven cases, could have involved three or more firms.

In three out of every five cases, firms from outside countries were involved: this proportion holds true whether it be the setting-up of simple subsidiaries or more complex operations. This trend has been dropping off slightly in the last few years. American firms, followed by British and Swiss firms, have predominated in all combinations involving outside countries; however, their share in such operations dropped sharply between 1966 and 1971.

Although the Japanese played a very small part in this movement a few years ago, their role is growing rapidly.

These cross-frontier reorganizations have very diverse effects on the various Community members, particularly if one takes into account the economic size of the country. For instance, Luxembourg has a lion's share, with 7 percent of all such operations; here, in effect, it is mostly a case of firms trying to take advantage of the very favorable tax conditions in the Grand Duchy.

France, Germany, and Belgium, each of which represents 23 percent of the total number of such reorganizations, all rank at the same level, which means that relatively five times as many such operations take place in Belgium as in the two larger countries; indeed, it is known that American firms show a marked preference for this country. With 12 percent, The Netherlands holds a middle position, probably because for a long time this country had bigger corporations than its Benelux neighbor. Italy ranks last, which shows that this country is the least integrated into the EEC.

Yet this picture of a spate of European combinations is too simplistic. It must be pointed out that the merger phenomenon has been at least as intense in the United States. Furthermore, it is rare that mergers of such scope take place across national boundaries. We scarcely see between different countries mergers like those that resulted in the establishment of Pechiney-Ugine-Kuhlmann or Saint-Gobain-Point-à-Mousson in France, or the setting up by Siemens and AEG-Telefunken of a joint subsidiary, KWD, for nuclear reactors in Germany. The Agfa-Gevaert merger remains an isolated case.

From one industry to another, changes in technical or legal structures have not resembled each other in either their speed or in the forms they have taken. These disparities are due primarily to the fact that the different groups of economic actors come into play with variable intensity.

Thus, it is tempting to classify the various economic activities according to the forms changes have taken under the influence of the Common Market. Obviously, such categories can only be approximate. Nevertheless, they can help to synthesize the developments of the last few years (and will further help, in Chapter Six, to outline the prospects for the future).

Four main categories of industries will now be discussed.

Semifinished and Consumer Goods

The economies of scale play an important part in industries producing semifinished and consumer goods. Notable examples in this category are various mechanical and electrical industries, chemicals, and steel. For all these products, the growth in intra-Community trade has been very considerable. Producers have clearly been seeking to secure an important place in the markets of the Community countries. This phenomenon, incidentally, came to the surface quite quickly after the signing of the Treaty of Paris for the steel industry and after the signing of the Treaty of Rome for the other industries. The leaders of the industries concerned did not wait until all customs barriers had been removed; they lost no time in setting up their marketing facilities. There are a number of indications that the same thing is going to happen between the Six and the three new members.

In some cases this expansion in trade was accompanied by genuine specialization. In some cases, on the other hand, it was advantageous for consumers, who profited from an extended range of products.

A few particularly representative cases will now be described.

TABLE 2.1

Household Electrical Appliances: Evolution of Output—Germany, France, Italy, The Netherlands and Belgium, 1958 and 1970
(thousands of appliances)

Country of Origin	Refrigerators		Washing Machines		TV sets	
	1958	1970	1958	1970	1958	1970
Germany	1,549	1,578	698	1,628	1,557	2,936
France	578	590	80	1,000	372	1,397
Italy	500	5,247	100	2,720	423	2,150
Netherlands	—	—	140	78	—	—
Belgium	7	22	(136)	(94)	—	504

Note: Figures in parentheses are approximations.
Source: SOEC and author's computations.

TABLE 2.2

Household Electrical Appliances: Evolution of the Share of Imports in
the Internal Supply—Germany, France, Italy, and The Netherlands, 1960 and 1970
(percent)

Country of Origin	Refrigerators		Washing Machines		TV sets	
	1960	1970	1960	1970	1960	1970
Germany	2.8	28.8	1.6	18.9	0.1	9.0
France	1.4	52.3	0.4	19.8	0.9	8.1
Italy	4.7	Є	4.7	Є	2.9	6.2
Netherlands	—	—	40.6	>70	—	—

Є stands for very small.

Source: SOEC and author's computations.

Household electrical goods offer an excellent example of the first case. Here, the development resulted in both an increase in production volume and in production transfers from one country to another, as well as in intensified concentration. (See Tables 2.1 and 2.2.)

The most extreme upheavals were recorded in the refrigerator industry. Whereas Germany and France in 1970 both produced the same number of appliances as in 1958—production had ceased in Belgium and The Netherlands—Italian production had increased tenfold during the same period. At the moment, Italy provides about 70 percent of Community production. This is one of the most dramatic examples of manufacturing specialization in one country.

This geographic shift in production was accompanied by a major change in production structures. Boldly committing themselves to this industry, Italian firms deliberately turned to long production runs. This choice forced other countries to adapt to the new circumstances: thus, the Siemens-Bosch amalgamation in Germany; the merger movement in France, which produced one manufacturer, Thomson-Brandt; and, finally, a halt in Benelux production. At present, the Italians are in a very strong position, thanks to the two giants Ignis and Zanussi-Zoppas, whose production easily surpasses that of the other European groupings.

In washing machines, the changes have been less extreme. For the quantities produced, however, the growth registered in Italian production has been every bit as dramatic, with half the Community production provided by the Italians. Yet, two other big countries have expanded their production of washing machines. The phenomenon of combination is much less advanced than for refrigerators: a certain balance has been reached between the Italian and German industries, while France, having had to face the fierce competition of its two neighbors, is now in a position to tackle foreign competition under better conditions, thanks to some recent mergers.

Lastly, in television sets, it is once again Italy that has greatly expanded its production. This time, however, its share of the Community market is much smaller (about 25 percent). Philips (and its subsidiaries) and a few German TV makers lead in the European market.

Sometimes it has been claimed that Italian household electrical goods are highly competitive because labor costs in Italy are lower than in other countries. Actually, the gaps between workers' wages in the different countries were smaller in electrical engineering than in manufacturing industries as a whole: in Germany, where workers earn the highest wages, hourly savings are lower in electrical engineering than in manufacturing industries as a whole, whereas in France and Italy, the reverse is true.

Moreover, the wage gaps between electrical engineering workers in the different EEC countries have been reduced. If one adds to the direct wage the other elements that make up the hourly cost of workers, there are only moderate differences between the two countries occupying the extreme positions: in 1969, the hourly cost of the Italian worker in electrical engineering went as high as 88 percent of the hourly cost of a German worker in the same industry. Thus, it is not the wage level that accounts for the boom in Italian exports.

In fact, here it is a question of consumer durables for which the number of buyers is great, and these buyers are not motivated by national preference. Formerly, the customs duties were often very high, and their elimination, and that of the quota restrictions which existed in some cases, were factors making for important changes, both in the production structures and in the location of producers. These changes were probably helped still further by the existence of a market that was growing very vigorously and in which the economies of scale could be utilized more easily. The Italians were particularly well placed to make the most of these two advantages at the same time, and they boldly gambled on very long-run productions, a bet they won—at least for some time.

Since the car industry was the first to demonstrate the advantages of mass production, it might have been expected that the Common Market was going to lead to an increased specialization of producers—either through mergers or through cooperative agreements—resulting in longer production runs and stepped-up productivity. However, there has not been anything like the upheavals met in the household electrical goods. Indeed, after 1958, the producers of cars in Community countries secured very big increases in their share of one another's markets. Taking the Community as a whole, the proportion of cars sold in a country other than that in which they were manufactured rose from 7 percent in 1958 to 31 percent in 1970.

In the same period, the share of cars from nonmember countries in the total new registrations only increased from 0.8 percent to 2.1 percent. However, these tendencies were in operation in practically all the Community countries, so that there was no revolutionary change in the comparative share of each producer in the total deliveries in Community territory. As for structural changes, those that have taken place consist mainly of longer production runs, and there has been little specialization (in some cases, indeed, the trend has been in the opposite direction); furthermore, there have been very few changes in the formal or legal organization of the industry.

Is the relative moderation of these changes due to the fact that the car industry had already reached a structure of equilibrium or to the interplay of factors that have held back any further changes?

According to certain studies, [6] one might distinguish two thresholds: one of around 250,000 cars per year and the second of around
1 million cars per year (enabling assembling to be automated). *

Among those firms that in 1958 were manufacturing less than
50,000 cars per year, several have been taken over (Lancia in Italy,
NSU and GLAS in Germany) and have not been able to survive, unlike
those linked to more powerful concerns (like Autobianchi) or that
have a special clientele (Porsche, Alfa-Romeo). It is the same for
firms producing between 50,000 and 100,000 cars, among which only
Daimler-Benz has experienced growth rapic enough to enable it to
maintain its autonomy.

Almost all the biggest producers are operating today: the only
major changes worth noting have been the Chrysler takeover of Simca
and Peugeot's takeover of Citröen (after the attempts made by Fiat
and Citröen to work together fell through).

There have been, therefore, considerable changes concerning
the small producers and rather few concerning the big producers, who
seem to be of the size where additional economies of scale are
slight.

Moreover, the thresholds mentioned above concern only the
technical optimum. They disregard social problems, which may be
connected with highly elaborate rationalizations (some firms are
beginning to wonder if it might not be necessary to revamp the organization of production in a way dramatically opposed to Taylorism
(for example, Volvo) and overlook the business risks that may result
from concentrating on one model or even one engine size).

Therein lies the main explanation for a phenomenon that was
not anticipated 20 years ago, that is, the increase in the number of
vehicle types available from each producer.

Finally, it must be pointed out that, unlike household electrical
goods, in the car industry the customers have tended to be faithful
and show, as well, a national preference. Even a certain regional
preference for local car manufacturers has been observed.

On the whole, developments in the last 15 years have brought
about a major increase in intra-Community trade and relatively
moderate changes in production structures.

Without a doubt, the consumer profits from a much wider range
of models (it is an open question how advantageous it is to have so

------

* Here, obviously, we are only dealing with approximation;
the annual production threshold also depends (to a great extent) on
the economic life of the model produced. It is the "length of the run"
that decides. If a firm can manage to change models less often than
its competitors, it may be very competitive with a lower annual production.

many models), and clearly, opening the borders favored a reduction in prices (in real terms). However, a certain price differentiation with respect to the country to which the goods are shipped does exist, a gap the Commission hopes to reduce by eliminating restrictions on re-export.

The producers played the Common Market game when it came to conquering member countries' markets, but have taken very few steps to cross borders to convert their production structures. Furthermore, the size attained by Common Market firms seems generally sufficient to profit from the majority of the economies of scale.

In the iron and steel industry, intra-Community trade has increased very sharply. In 1954, it represented 11 percent of Community production; the proportion has been increasing consistently and is now around 20 percent. The trend toward combination in this industry has been intensive during the past decade; this can be seen in the fact that 70 percent of Community production now comes from 8 groups of firms, compared with 15 groups in 1958. It is to be noted, nevertheless, that the mergers have taken place entirely between companies in the same country, save in one case—that of the German-Dutch Hoesch-Hoogovens. There is, incidentally, no reason for thinking that reorganization of the iron and steel industry, involving many more cross-frontier mergers, would have resulted in a more efficient reorganization of the production machine. The pooling of the iron and steel industries of the Six was, in 1951, essentially a political act, at a time when steel production was considered both as a motivating force for the whole economy and an industry vital to national defense. Under both these heads, the comparative importance of this industry has greatly diminished.

As a first approximation, it is estimated that the industries which have passed through the type of development illustrated in these three examples account for nearly half the Community's industrial activity.

Industries with National and Local Markets

Quite a number of industries have been much less affected by the Common Market. These comprise in the first instance certain industries in which the individual firms cope with markets that are comparatively localized or which cannot easily enter into external trade. These industries are characterized by the large number of buyers and the relative paucity of government purchases. Generally, the state intervenes little—or not at all—in their development. Likewise, if many of them have undergone rapid growth, these are still not what are usually called "peak industries" or "high technology industries." Research and development is kept at a low level, with few exceptions, and major technological transformations are infrequent.

The clearest instance is the building industry, in which the technological development of the past 15 years, which has certainly been far from negligible, has not been materially influenced by the opening of frontiers. Admittedly, the vigorous expansion in the building trade owes much to the increase of purchasing power and, thus, indirectly to the existence of the Common Market; but even in the pooling of experiences and research to resolve problems that arise in similar terms in every country, the progress made has been extremely modest, and neither the national nor the Community authorities have yet made any tangible effort to improve matters.

The construction industry, and the other industrial branches that fall in the same category, represent about a third of Community industry.

Other industries under this heading have sought, by some degree of concerted practice, to keep their share of the market in approximately the same balance as before, and thus bypass the effects of increased competition. One of the most recent examples of this was provided by the chief Community sugar producers, who sought to guarantee the strength of one another's position in their respective national markets and preserve for themselves in those markets the control of the marketing of sugar for human consumption.

It seems, indeed, that the proportion of Community industry which has followed this line of action is quite small; however, the significance of these cases is great because such pockets of illegality set a bad example.

Public Tenders

There is a group of industries that benefits by a particular interest from national governments, which take a special interest in these industries, either because they are buyers of a large part of the production or because these industries are considered strategically important from the standpoint of long-term economic development. For the most part, they are industries in which the initial research and development expenditure must be particularly great and in which extensive financial backing is, therefore, a particularly important asset. They are also industries in which big multinational firms play an especially important part.

The mere opening of the internal borders of the Common Market is not enough to produce appreciable changes for these industries.

On the one hand, the customs barriers can in large measure be by-
passed by setting up subsidiaries in those countries where the firms
concerned are seeking to secure a market; and on the other hand,
they are industries for which public orders are an appreciable part
of the market. National preferences form an obstacle to the conquest
of this market that is far more formidable than customs duties.

It is thus easy to understand why the simple elimination of
trade barriers has not given rise to great structural changes. What
has been lacking is agreement at Community level: (1) on the thorough
liberalization of public-contract awards, (2) on a joint research and
development and innovation effort in specific branches of industry, and
(3) on a common attitude about the structural reorganizations that
are desirable and the part foreign companies should be encouraged
to play. As a result, the only important action taken has consisted
in intergovernment agreements on aircraft manufacture—but even
then without cross-frontier mergers—or has been the work of multinational firms in the data-processing sector.

The data-processing sector expanded and became a top-level
industry precisely during the years the Common Market was being
set up.* Have the computer producers taken advantage of the opportunities offered by this Common Market and this elimination of
customs duties to build (at the outset) an industry of European scale?
The answer varies with the firms considered.

One corporation has taken full advantage of this opportunity by
setting up at least one factory in each of the important countries of
Western Europe and by splitting up its production on the basis of
one product for one factory; but all the various activities are coordinated in the general strategy planned in New York at the IBM head
office.

A second corporation, also American, holds a far from unimportant place in the European market as a whole. This corporation's
success is due to the fact that European countries have twice abandoned
the opportunity (first, on the national level, and second, on a broader
level) to use a French firm in financial difficulty as the nucleus from
which to launch a corporation of European scale. This is Honeywell-
Bull, created by General Electric's (GE's) takeover of the French
Bull in 1964, then by Honeywell's takeover of this corporation in

---

* It was around 1956 that the second generation of computers
using transistors appeared, represented by International Business
Machine (IBM's) 7090 and 1401. Between 1962 and 1967, the number
of computers installed in the Community of Nine increased eightfold
and those in the United States fivefold.

1970, and lastly, in 1975, by Honeywell-Bull's merger with CII (Compagnie Internationale pour l'informatique).

Other European corporations are much smaller, except for ICL in the United Kingdom and work primarily for the national market. [*]

Given that European firms have found it impossible to continue to exist or to expand in the face of competition from American firms, several European governments have found it necessary to step in. The first intervention was that of the French government in drawing up the Plan Calcul ("Computer Plan"). For the period of 1966 to 1970, the Plan Calcul brought into play the equivalent of 130 million units of account (ua); a second five-year Plan Calcul was later established). In the United Kingdom, the ICL corporation resulted from a series of mergers and associations, first as a private undertaking and then, following 1965, with the help of a government subsidy. Lastly, in Germany, the government came up with grants and loans to the tune of 74 million ua between 1967 and 1971, and then, in 1972, a new five-year plan was launched.

For the last 10 years, these government interventions have been characterized mainly by their strictly national approach. At the Community level, attempts have been made on a rather modest scale to promote mergers between European firms, particularly producers of central processing units, such as AEG (Telefunken) and Siemens in Germany, CII in France, Philips in The Netherlands, ICL in the United Kingdom, and the big producer of peripheral units, Olivetti in Italy. These attempts were first started in 1969 by way of an ambitious research and development project that aimed at perfecting a high-capacity data-processing system using completely advanced technology. But due to the unwillingness of the firms to take on such a prospect and the equal unwillingness of the governments to commit themselves to such massive financing, nothing was accomplished. The last few years have been characterized by many conversations between two or three firms.

Different attempts at partial agreements have been considered. The most far-reaching was the one known as Unidata, which associated Siemens, Philips, and CII. But the 1975 merger of CII and Honeywell-Bull dealt what is probably a final blow to this agreement. This marks, moreover, a turning point in French policy in this field, which preferred a Franco-American agreement to a European one.

---

[*] In the Community market as a whole, IBM holds 60 percent of the market and other American producers 20 percent, with ICL holding 10 percent and other European producers another 10 percent.

Seeing the limited effects of its interventions, the Commission proceeded to put forward a proposal laying out the basic elements of a medium-term program (1977-80). [7] This proposal is in keeping with the Council's resolution of July 15, 1974, regarding a Community policy for dataprocessing, which had as its purpose to lay the foundation of an industrial policy in this sector.

This proposal provides for the Community financing of a second set of development projects, amounting to 25 million ua. The main goals are standardization, including the development of a common programming language and softward capable of being used regardless of the make of computer; the perfecting of data protection methods; and the expansion of dataprocessing in the field of documentary research.

Lastly, the proposal defines a medium-term program to support industry in such a way as to guarantee equal competition conditions (with the objective of securing 41 percent of the market for Community firms in the leasing field by 1979 and 50 percent by 1985). This program also aims at making it easier to benefit from the economies of scale in areas where these are necessary, (especially in the field of peripheral units and terminals).

However interesting these actions, they are only modest in scope and are not really equal to the problem. So far, the data-processing sector seems like the sector of lost opportunities.

The aircraft industry is a sector where intra-European cooperation experienced rather impressive growth in the 1960's. Unfortunately, the effects of this cooperation have been limited. First, this cooperation was more in the stages of development and wholesale manufacture than in the marketing stages, although it was in the latter field that the need for a pooling of existing capacities was most obvious. Second, this policy of cooperation often brought conflicting interests into play, since each country retained its interests in other civil and military programs, which were often at odds with the interests of the other countries it was in cooperation with (for example, the Airbus project was launched without the participation of the United Kingdom, although, at the same time, Rolls Royce was working with Lockheed on the Tristar, and there is the marked absence of France in the Multiple Range Combat Aircraft).

Here again, the aircraft industry provides an example of lost opportunities: faced with the conflicts stemming from national policies, in October 1975, the Commission proposed "an action program for the European aircraft industry" that revealed a wish to go beyond the stage of national aircraft policies and, for this, advocated that the Community oversee the development of the aircraft industry. [8] No decision has yet been made.

Thus, in a group of industries dominated by government orders, any reorganizations that have taken place have almost never been of the cross-frontier type. Admittedly, the industries in question represent only a modest percent of all industrial activity. A few years ago, the part they could play in the economy was somewhat over-estimated, and there is now a return to a more balanced idea of the mechanisms of industrial growth. They could, nevertheless, be very valuable as pacemakers for the whole economy by promoting rapid innovation, and it is this that makes them important. More-over, most of them are of the type in which substantial economies of scale can be achieved through specialization in individual firms and through longer production runs, in which the national market is often too small (the aircraft industry) and in which national efforts fall far short of what is needed (dataprocessing, where the 30 million to 50 million ua per year of the national Calcul plans is far off the 500 million to 800 million ua that perfecting the IBM 360 computer range would have cost).

Here, therefore, we have a case where the changeover to a plurinational or Community level might turn out to be especially beneficial.

COMMON POLICIES

In two sectors, the energy sector and agriculture, and in one field, scientific and technical research, attempts have been made to work out common ideas at the Community level and to decide on and carry out tasks in common. The results have varied, and an analysis of these attempts clearly illuminates the decision-making mechanisms in the Community. Taking this into account, the following developments have bearing beyond the few cases under consideration.

Energy

Here is a field that has been a major concern since the begin-ning of Community construction and where, 25 years later, there is still no real common coal market, nor real common market for other energy sources, nor, even less, an overall energy policy.

One is led to ask why it has so far been impossible to come to a satisfactory result in such an important field.

Since the beginning of European construction, the importance of the energy problem has been acknowledged and reacknowledged many times:[*] in 25 years, two specific treaties and two

---

[*]The following were the major steps taken to deal with this

intergovernment protocols have been signed, a dozen or so recommendations by the High Authority or the Commission have been made to the Council, and some basic energy studies, which rank high in the opinion of foreign observers, have been made.

Furthermore, during the same period, the general energy situation went through two turnarounds:

_____

problem:

1. 1951: The signing of the Treaty establishing the European Coal and Steel Community took place.

2. 1957: The signing of the Euratom Treaty occurred. The Treaty of Rome did not cover a Community energy policy, but as of October 1957, the Council of Ministers adopted a protocol on the means to ensure a coordinated policy in the energy field.

3. 1960: In March, the Energy Interexecutive Group sent the Council a provisional communication on energy policy, the major point of which was a "guideline price." The Council did not accept the communication or the two proposed programs of priority actions that came a little later.

4. 1962: In June, the Interexecutive Group presented its memorandum on energy policy, which proposed an open Common Market, moderated by a concerted policy at the Community level. It was rejected by the Council.

5. 1964: On April 21, a protocol concerning energy problems was adopted by the governments of the member states. It dealt primarily with problems of coal and was very modest in scope.

6. 1966: First communication on Community policy on oil and natural gas was presented.

7. 1967: In July, the Council of Ministers took note of this memorandum by issuing First General Guidelines for Community Policy in the Field of Oil and Natural Gas.

8. 1968: In December, there was a new Commission communication to the Council on the urgency of an oil policy.

9. 1972: In October, there were Commission communications to the Council on "the Means and the Problems of the Energy Policy for the Period of 1975 to 1985" and on "The Necessary Progress of the Community Energy Policy," which defined the general principles of an energy policy.

10. 1973: In April, there was another Commission communication on "Guidelines and Priority Actions for the Community Energy Policy."

11. 1974: In May, the Commission put forward new proposals: "Towards a New Energy Policy Strategy for the Community."

1. Between 1950 and 1958, there were difficulties in supply (because of problems with the balance of payments), with prospects of a shortage and a price bribe. The Suez crisis brought the dominating role played by oil once again to the surface.

2. Between 1959 and 1971, the supply of oil on the world market was large and at low prices, with an outlook for stability in technical prices.

3. Since 1971, there have been oil problems, an end both to the abundance and the low price (an increase in oil royalties), competition between the great powers on the international energy market, and a shift toward a situation of scarcer and more expensive energy.

Since 1960, Community oil production has stayed at the same level, while its dependence on foreign sources rose from 32 percent to 63 percent in 1973.

Amid all these declarations and changes in the energy situation, one thing stands out as a constant—the impossibility of reaching an agreement on a Community policy of any major scope. Up until now, it has proved impossible to go further than the agreement that aims at getting around the prohibition decreed by the ECSC Treaty against government coal production subsidies, the occasional confrontations on the energy situation and the different national measures taken, and an agreement on the maximum level of oil stockpiling.

On the other hand, no decision at all has been made on a course of action to take toward countries outside the EEC.

Thus, despite a rapid rise in oil consumption, the Community continues to depend on international oil companies (especially, American firms). The EEC constitutes the world's biggest oil buyer, but things are settled without seeking Europe's opinion.

How was this point reached? There had been no lack of warnings In 1957, the Objectif pour Euratom, a report drawn up under the direction of Louis Armand, stressed the coming fragility in the European energy supply: from this resulted the Euratom Treaty. In 1962-64, the Commission Study on the Long-Term Energy Outlook for the EEC, much read because it tackled the problem of the evolution in costs and prices, again pointed out the risks Europe faced in its energy supply in the way of prices and of quantity.

In 1968, the Commission once again raised the overall problem of energy by emphasizing future dangers. Finally, a 1972 document showed that the circumstances of energy policy had considerably changed since 1969 and would continue to do so in the coming years. The causes of this indecisiveness can be found in the very different attitudes of the member countries toward the priorities of an energy policy, as well as the ways of action. This diversity of attitudes can be explained both by serious differences in the energy situation of each EEC country and by differences in the general conception of an internal and external economic policy.

Above all, it is in the interest of the Community to secure the availability of supplies of oil at relatively stable prices and as cheaply as possible, since social or regional policies may lead to a slowdown or a speed-up in the process of natural substitution (replacement of coal by oil).[9] These are partly contradictory objectives and what is most important varies greatly from country to country.

If one looks at the energy situation in 1960, one finds that the Community of Six falls into three categories: Italy and The Netherlands are supplied primarily through crude oil imports; Belgium and Germany use mainly national coal resources; and France occupies a position between the two, producing considerable coal and yet importing rather large amounts of crude oil.

Additional factors played their part in complicating the situation. Toward 1960, the production cost of coal was much higher than the cost of imported coal in Belgium, slightly lower in France, and average in Germany. Thus, national coal production could only be maintained either through protectionism, or through state subsidies. These subsidies were large in Belgium and rather sizable in France; in Germany, however, in 1960, the problem did not arise.

As for The Netherlands, they have one of the seven biggest oil companies and very large reserveds in the Middle East. Thus, for them, the problem of a continuous supply is not crucial. Italy has long tended to think that there is no problem of the availability of supplies for a country that, around 1960, only imported 3 percent of the world oil production. France, on the other hand, has a long tradition of government oil policy, which dates back to the Law of 1928. After the Second World War, France undertook a great research effort in North Africa and in the Sahara, which was partly successful from the technical standpoint. For France, a continued availability of oil supply remains of overriding importance.

We must remember that as far as general economic policy is concerned, Germany and The Netherlands are opposed to interventionist measures, France is more open to them, and Italy and Belgium take a middle-of-the-road position, depending on the problems and the situation at the time.

Finally, if government intervention existed, it has only figured as part of foreign policy reserved for the jealously guarded reserve of the state governments.

Thus, the shortsightedness of the Council of Ministers over the past few years, which is responsible for the current situation, may be explained (if not excused) by the following points:

1. Each minister finds it difficult to consider problems from an overall Community standpoint. At the national level, if there is

a break in supply from any area of the world (such as the one France and the United Kingdom briefly experienced in 1956), it can be mitigated by falling back on another source. But what is possible for one country (and 3 percent of world oil) is not possible for nine countries that use one-quarter of the world oil production and import from the Middle Eastern Arab countries more than half the total world oil exports. As is often the case in economics, aggregation changes the nature of the problem.*

2. The various countries' economic philosophy has led them to rely too much on the mechanisms of foreign trade and private enterprise. (However, it has not been proved that direct negotiations between consumer states and producer states would have been more effective.)

3. By postponing (more than provided for in the Treaty) the working out of a common commercial policy, it became impossible to put the problem of energy supply in its proper place in the general context of relations with the rest of the world.

4. Lastly, the Europeans were naive enough to believe that the Organization of Petroleum Exporting Countries (OPEC) countries would behave much like European countries and would have as much trouble as the EEC countries in acting together with a common policy. The blow that hit in fall 1973 made the European countries more aware of their vulnerability. Not only did they depend physically on the goodwill of OPEC, but the tripling or quadrupling of the price of energy made their economies less competitive compared to countries that were only moderate importers, like the United States. Thus, in its May 1974 communication, the Commission presented new proposals moving in the direction of a Community energy policy. "The new strategy" aims at changing the Community's energy supply structure in order to reduce its dependence on imported energy (to 50 percent, and to 40 percent if possible, by 1985, instead of 63 percent in 1973) and particularly on imported oil (to 75 percent in 1985 instead of 98 percent in 1973).

Lastly, in a communication to the Council in January 1976, the Commission reminded the Council of its proposals regarding the solidarity of member countries in case of difficulties with the oil supply, as well as energy-saving programs and the protection and development of internal energy resources, and asked the Council to adopt these "without further delay."

---

* It is intriguing to note that it was The Netherlands, the country least convinced about the importance of taking action to secure a steady supply of oil, which underwent the first restrictions in 1973.

If the Council has scarcely taken any action, it is because the
diversity of national attitudes persists. The widening of the Community
brought in one country, the United Kingdom, which hopes to become
self-sufficient if indeed not an exporter due to its North Sea finds, and
thus sees its interest as lying in high oil prices. Also, the international strategy varies from country to country, particularly on the
kind of dialogue to undertake with the oil-producing countries and on
to what extent it is advisable or not to line up with the strategy of the
United States.

Agriculture

In all industrialized countries, governments intervene in favor
of the agricultural sector, at the very least to stabilize the prices
of agricultural produce in relation to crop variations and, most
often, to ensure the farmers an income in keeping with the rest of the
population.

The low level of farmer income in many areas is the result of
too many agricultural workers; inevitably, it is only in reducing this
number and reorganizing operations that, in time, a rise in the standard of living comes about. The number of people employed in agriculture in the Community of Six decreased by 21 percent between
1960 and 1965, and again as much in the five years following, or by
one-half between 1958 and 1972, reaching about 8.6 million at the
end of that time. The Mansholt Plan of 1968 hoped to reduce this to
5 million workers by 1980, and proposed a level of equilibrium of
3 million to 3.5 million workers around the year 2000,[*] or 4.5 percent to 5 percent of the total active population.

At the time the Treaty of Rome was being worked out, two
attitudes were possible: (1) given the special circumstances in agriculture, to keep agricultural produce outside the effective scope of
the Treaty and to let each member country follow its own agricultural
policy, or (2) to provide for the setting up of a common policy.

Since food prices played such an important role in the general
level of prices, it was feared that a coexistence of clearly different
agricultural policies from one country to the next might distort competition for nonagricultural goods and activities. Moreover, it seemed
a good idea to gradually move toward a better distribution of productions throughout Community territory; also, certain countries were

---

[*] In the Community of Nine, the active agricultural population
amounted to 9.1 million people in 1974, or 8.9 percent of the total
active population.

very interested in being able to export their produce all over the
Common Market.

For all these reasons, agricultural produce was included in
the Common Market, and a common agricultural policy was provided. *

Despite these particularly favorable conditions—which have not
been found in other fields where common policies have been attempted—
it has taken 10 years to work out an agricultural policy.

The fact that all member countries shared the same basic philosophy provided favorable circumstances. First, in every country,
measures existed that aimed at promoting reorganizations. Second,
and above all, a rise in farmers' incomes was sought everywhere by
the means of upholding farm prices, but not by directly transferring
incomes over to the farmers, as was done in the United Kingdom.
Therefore, quite naturally, it was proposed to carry this out on a
general level and in a uniform manner.

As of December 1959, the Commission sent a memorandum to
the Council, of which the following lines were the crux:

"In the long run, agricultural problems can only be solved by a complete reorganization and improvement of the agricultural structures.
The accomplishment of such a project presupposes the development
of the general economic structure of agricultural regions."[10] The
interaction between agricultural policy, general economic policy,
and regional development policy was thus clearly recognized.

Since the effects of a structural improvement policy would only
be felt after some time, a market policy was necessary to reach the
Treaty's objectives.

The basic conception was thus rather well balanced, with the
stress placed on structural changes.

Slowly, this system came into effect. On January 14, 1962, the
Council made a series of decisions concerning the common organization

---

* According to the terms set out in Article 39, the goals were:

1. to increase agricultural productivity by promoting technical progress and by ensuring the rational development of agricultural production and the optimum utilization of the factors of production, in
particular, labor;
2. to ensure a fair standard of living for the agricultural community,
in particular by increasing the individual earnings of persons engaged
in agriculture;
3. to stabilize markets;
4. to assure the availability of supplies; and
5. to ensure that supplies reach consumers at reasonable prices.

of agricultural markets and the setting up of the EAGGF (European Agricultural Guidance and Guarantee Fund).

For the organization of markets, the procedure is relatively complicated. The basic factor is the target price, that is, the probable price in the marketing center of the area within the Community with the most adverse budget balance. At the frontier of the Community, the threshold price is subtracted, with adjustments for transport costs. A charge is levied on imports equal to the difference between the threshold price and the CIF (Cost Insurance Freight) price. The intervention price is the price at which intervention organizations are required to buy at any moment if the market price tends to undergo a further drop. Actually, the intervention price is 5 percent to 10 percent lower than the target price. At times of exports to outside markets at world prices below the intervention prices, the buyer is compensated to make up for the difference. Last, guaranteed prices may come into play for the entire production, regardless of its size, or for a limited amount. Also, a Community system of equalization of storage prices may be put into effect.

It took some time to bring prices among the different countries into line. *

As for the redirection of agricultural structures, the bases of intervention of the guidance section of the EAGGF were laid out in 1964, but the expenditure only reached an appreciable level three or four years later (17 million ua in 1965, 80 million ua in 1967, 200 million ua in 1969, and 243 million ua in 1971). Until 1968, the amounts available went as high as one-third of the expenditure of the guarantee section. But in 1969, due to the considerable rise in costs of the markets policy, the Council decided to limit the amounts for redirection to 285 million ua (325 million ua as of January 1973 due to the widening of the EEC). Thus, the credits committed to redirection only amounted to 10 percent of the total commitments of the EAGGF from 1965 to 1974. And, as a matter of fact, these sums were not even spent. This shift in the use of funds seriously distorts the general mechanism of the agricultural policy and has mortgaged the medium-term reorganization actions to the benefit of short-term objectives. †

---

* The step-by-step implementation of single prices followed this schedule: November 11, 1966—olive oil; July 1, 1967—grains, pork, poultry and eggs, fruits and vegetables; September 1, 1967—rice; July 1, 1968—beets and sugar; July 29, 1968—dairy products and beef; and June 1, 1970—wines.

† Setting up the EAGGF has not eliminated national public aids to agriculture: in 1975, these reached 9.4 billion ua, as opposed to

Furthermore, faced with soaring guarantee expenses, the Commission proposed as early as 1968 (that is, just after single prices began to be put into practice) to change the agricultural policy: the Mansholt Plan suggested stressing structural reforms and reorienting the EAGGF toward this type of intervention. Although these proposals gave rise to many impassioned debates and seemed to be looked on rather favorably by young farmers, they were only partly put into effect in the three decisions of the Council (April 1972) concerning the modernization of farms, actions to encourage the ceasing of agricultural activity, and social economic information and the professional qualifications of persons engaged in agriculture.

It is difficult to make a judgment on the common agricultural policy, since the qualitative objectives announced by the Treaty, which may prove contradictory, have never been clearly defined in quantitative terms.

First, what has happened to the "fair income" objective? From the outset, it must be noted that the idea of income may mean many things. If we speak of the value added per worker, the gap between agricultural and other activities is slight in Belgium and The Netherlands (as well as in the United Kingdom and in Denmark) and great in other countries. Thus, there are two different groups of countries in the Community. And this gap has not been narrowed in any appreciable way in the last 15 years.

But things look entirely different if one takes the available family income; then one finds that, in Germany in 1969, this income was more than 20 percent higher for a farming family than for a nonfarming family; in France in 1969, total consumption for a family was the same for a farming family and a nonfarming family. This is due to the fact that the number of persons in a farming family is greater in Germany (four as against three in France), and thus, there are more incomes in the family (from farming or other sources).

In particular, ideas of national average are surprisingly misleading. Just from one region to the next, the disparities are great. Thus the ratio of gross domestic product (GDP) per agricultural assets and per nonagricultural assets, which is 0.37 percent for all of Germany, goes as high as 0.72 percent for Schleswig-Holstein and drops to 0.27 percent in Bavaria. In Italy, the extremes are 0.76 percent and 0.32 percent. In France, using a very different indicator (gross agricultural holding income per assets), the differences range from 1.78 percent to 0.39 percent.

4.9 for the EAGGF; taken together these aids represent 21 percent of the value of final agricultural production. See "The Agricultural Situation in the Community," Report 1975.

TABLE 2.3

Labor Income per Work-Year Unit, EEC
1970-71
(units of account)

Size of Agricultural Undertaking in Hectares	Arable Land	Stock Breeding	Fruit Growing	Wine Growing	Total
5-10	760	1,380	2,190	2,070	1,420
10-20	1,400	1,580	2,720	3,480	1,650
20-50	2,380	1,980	4,190	3,040	2,088
50	4,720	2,220	—	—	3,280

Source: Réseau d'information comptable agricole.

These regional disparities are largely the result of income
differences, according to farm sizes and kinds of produce (see Table
2.3). After years of agricultural policy, there are still huge disparities in income, a fact that justifies the harshness of some of the
criticisms which have been made.[11] By means of raising incomes
through prices, small- or medium-sized farms located on soil of
average fertility are just as favored as the big farms in the most
fertile regions of the Community. These disparities in fertility,
which are already sizable at the national level, become more so at
the Community level, since the area is large. The fixing of farm
prices by the Council is the result of a compromise, wherein each
member aims at safeguarding the income of its poorest farmers, an
approach that, despite the Commission's efforts, leads to a price
structure which sets up sizable differential rents for some farmers,
surpluses for some produce (wheat and milk), and deficits for other
products (such as beef).

The second objective, the availability of supplies, has never
been much talked about. It must be admitted that since the capacity
of the Community of Six to provide for itself was considerable, it
was hardly a problem.[*] For the Nine, things are a bit different, and
the alert given by the energy crisis should lead to a more serious
consideration of this aspect.

As for judging the "reasonable" nature of the price to the consumer, this is a difficult task. Should one compare European prices
with world prices? If so, when one sees European prices two or
three times higher than world prices, one is tempted to say they
are very unreasonable.[†] But these world prices are often valid for
a very small fraction of world production and, thus, may undergo
great fluctuations. Because of this, they are hardly meaningful.
Furthermore, at the turn of 1974, world prices for many products
(wheat, rice, sugar, and so forth) were higher than Community
prices.

In fact, the idea of a "reasonable price" has two aspects: it is
linked to the idea of availability of supply, and it reflects an option
with regard to the margin of support for farm incomes and the

---

[*] To demonstrate this, the figures were more than 100 percent
for wine; around 100 percent for wheat, potatoes, dairy products,
and meat; around 90 percent for grains as a whole, sugar, butter,
and vegetables; 80 percent for fruits; and 40 percent for citrus fruits
and fats and oils as a whole.

[†] In 1968, the ratio of prices on the Community market and
on the world market reached 185 for soft wheat, 400 for butter and
sugar and 175 for beef.

insurance premium. The latter may be made by the price paid by the consumer or by levying a tax (as in the United Kingdom). It is probable that both methods do not hit the various citizens equally. The idea of a reasonable price to the consumer can only be judged by taking into account agriculture alone, and the choice must be based on a comprehensive idea of income distribution in the economy as a whole.

Last, one may wonder whether throughout Community territory, the various regions have tended to become specialized in produce for which they are relatively most efficient.

An overall analysis shows a certain trend toward relocation of produce within the EEC according to the demands of the division of labor. Thus, the rate of growth of intra-Community trade in agricultural produce since 1963 (409) has been over the rate for all product trade (375). At the same time, the relative share of regulated agricultural produce in intra-Community exports increased greatly between 1965 and 1973 for Germany (9.6 percent to 13.5 percent), France (27.7 percent to 33.3 percent), and the BLEU (11.6 percent to 13.8 percent), whereas it took a major drop for Italy (from 16.1 percent to 9 percent) and The Netherlands (from 40 percent to 30.6 percent).

However, an analysis at the level of products themselves gives quite different results and leads us to moderate our conclusions: a certain rigidity in the regional sites of crop production is noticed, whereas there has been a marked shift of egg and poultry production toward the consuming centers.

The information currently at hand does not make it possible to assess the rational nature of these movements. Actually, the experts scarcely seem to agree on the optimum sites, particularly if one goes into some detail. However, a few distortions can be observed between different countries: between 1963 and 1970, crop production rose 23 percent in the Community, but by 36 percent in France and 40 percent in The Netherlands; overall livestock breeding rose by 27 percent, but by 43 percent in Italy and The Netherlands. At first sight, these movements seem reasonable.

Consequently, we see that the agricultural policy has followed the same road as the national policies: planned at the beginning with some sort of balance, it backed price guarantees to meet the most immediate demands, and only when these guarantees became a heavy financial burden did serious efforts at complete farm reorganization and a cutback in the work force begin to be considered. But opposing interests in different countries make this evolution difficult—each country wishes to keep a few prices high (Germany its wheat, France its milk, and Italy its rice and olive oil, and so forth). The necessary planning might take the two following forms: (1) more measures to

promote the reorganization of structures (the decisions of March
1972, January 1974, and February 1975 were a first step in this
direction); and (2) less use of the policy of price-supported incomes
and greater use of specific subsidies to farmers or former farmers
in the lowest income brackets.

Here, public funds would be used essentially to attain social
and structural objectives, while prices would have as their main
function to orient productions in such a way as to avoid surpluses,
while maintaining the necessary level of European production.

The latest proposals have been along this line. The Commission,
in its memorandum of October 31, 1973,

> opted for a division of labor between these two policies
> (price policy and structural policy). It based its price
> proposals partly on the real income needs of farms
> which have reached the point where they are profitable,
> and left to structural policy the task of bringing as
> many other farms as possible up to this point.

It remains to better the income of farmers who cannot reach this
point. A first move was made in 1975 in favor of mountain farmers
and backward agricultural areas. Others will have to follow.

In entering the Community, the United Kingdom accepted the
conditions of the common agricultural policy in force among the
Six, but this did not stop it from later seeking to have these amended.
However, the rise in world prices (and, particularly, American
prices) brought home the fact that a certain Community supply was
to its interest.

As a matter of fact, this provides one more case of a certain
duality between those countries that receive more from the EAGGF
than they contribute to it (France, The Netherlands, and Denmark)
and those in the contrary position (particularly Germany), who
would like to see a slowdown in the growing expenditure of EAGGF.

Research and Development

Curiously enough, problems of research have been treated
quite differently in the different European treaties. Whereas the
Treaty of Paris explicitly provides for Community action in research
in the coal and steel sectors (Article 55), and the Treaty of Rome,
in setting up Euratom, aims at organizing all nuclear research in
the Community, the EEC Treaty does not explicitly raise the problems
of research and development (except for Article 41 on agricultural
research). This lack of any explicit reference in the Treaty of Rome
to the Community tasks in research and development has held us back.

Coal and Steel Industries: A Limited Success

There were two objectives: (1) to promote a certain degree of integration in research under way in the various countries, whether carried on by firms or by professional associations; and (2) to reorient research efforts in what seemed the most important direction.

Since 1955, the funds allocated by the ECSC to research projects in the iron and steel industries have represented an average of 12 percent and 4 percent of all expenditure devoted to research in the member states.

The granting of funds by the ECSC certainly stimulated an intensification of research projects. On the other hand, there has been no real change in direction toward high-priority projects, because at the Community level, there is no real method of selecting priority projects, and also because resources have been spread out over a large number of subjects.

The Nuclear Field: Complete Lack of Success

In 1958, nuclear development in Europe was still at a rather modest stage, except in two countries, France and the United Kingdom. It was to be hoped that, at the Community level, many tasks could be coordinated and, in certain cases, even carried out more rapidly than in traditional, well-established activities.

In practice, however, Euratom soon failed to function smoothly due to the appearance of different viewpoints among the member countries. Although the first four-year program provided for in the Treaty developed satisfactorily, difficulties emerged with the second, and it has never been possible to come to an agreement on a follow-up program. Work has thus been carried out without a long-term over-all plan.

For research and educational programs, the outlay has amounted to aroung 1 billion ua since 1958. Technological research in connection with the development of reactors accounts for about 70 percent of the total (with a clear drop these last few years), activities in the public utilities sector for 20 percent, and guided basic research for 10 percent. A part of this money went to the organizations of the Euratom Common Research Center, the rest to contracts and associations arranged with Euratom.

As regards the tasks of coordination and collaboration in the sectors of basic research (fusion and biology for example) there were positive and appreciable results, whereas they were far more incomplete in development programs of a technological nature.

As for research carried out at the Joint Research Center, apart from the technical results themselves (of universally admitted high quality) the consequences of these projects have remained incomplete to the extent that these projects have not been incorporated into a comprehensive strategy of development for an industry integrated at the Community level. To the contrary, under the pressure applied by the Member States, technical success has not been able to prevent (or has even brought about) a strengthening of particularism. This especially holds true for the crucial sector of breeders reactors.

For its part, the Orgel project has not been able to find its place in a coherent development policy for heavy water moderated reactors, although the Community has allocated major funds to this project. This situation primarily stems from the fact that several member countries have committed themselves to developing various types of the heavy water moderated reactor outside the collaboration proposed by the Commission and for which it set up an ad hoc work group in 1959. [12]

The total nuclear expenditure over 15 years (Community and national) has not been less than that allocated to the same field in the United States in the same period. Indeed, in 1958, Europe was far behind the United States, but we were entitled to expect, on the basis of this comparison, major results in the development of European lines. What is the current situation?

At the beginning, the European gas-graphite line of reactors was used; power plants currently under construction are based on lines of American origin, built in Europe under license.

Of course, a research effort was needed in any case if foreign techniques were to be put to use effectively and if they were to be gradually Europeanized (so that, little by little, Europe could escape from foreign technological tutelage). Nevertheless, without any doubt, the efforts undertaken fell far short of what was needed: large sums were devoted to perfecting a line that works technically but which, from an economic standpoint, is doomed.

In 1958, there were two possible avenues open to Europe: (1) to decide to carry out a large-scale research effort to perfect a European solution, but to concentrate this effort on one proved reactor line—or a maximum of two—(more active research on breeder reactors); and (2) to consent to a more moderate nuclear effort and intentionally work with the United States, concentrating on attempts to rapidly assimilate and gradually Europeanize these imported technique

There was a certain logic to both these approaches, but likewise, both would have had better chances of success if they had been
adopted by all the EEC countries. As it is, both directions were taken
at the same time. At the beginning, one country, France (like the
United Kingdom outside the EEC), concentrated all its efforts on the
natural uranium gas-graphite line so as to be independent of the American uranium-enrichment plants for fuel supplies (since the costs of
building a European plant seemed prohibitive at that time). At the same
time, Euratom concluded an agreement with the United States to work
on developing light-water nuclear plants (the expenses to be borne
equally by both), using enriched uranium. Then, later, Euratom
committed itself to research on the heavy-water line.

Even if it is admitted that the gas-graphite line had built-in
reasons to be more costly than the uranium-enriched line, it is
equally certain that it was the lack of coordination of research in
Community territory and the lack of a close and rapid research
collaboration that compromised the chances of this line. From the
moment when there were only two types of enriched uranium reactors
in the United States and many in Europe, the European solutions were
doomed in advance.

Several lessons are to be learned from this experience that are
applicable to other very high technology sectors. In technological
matters, it is naive to think that a priori only one technical solution
is possible and that it is, in a way, "Godgiven." Usually, several
solutions emerge from the beginning, all equally technologically
feasible and economically similar, but the mere choice of one and the
concentration of all efforts in that direction gives it a certain glitter,
which cannot be removed thereafter.

A double-threshold effect comes into play for a minimum number of efforts in research and development and design perfection as
well as for the orders that are later placed. On the other hand, rather
than wanting to "rediscover" solutions already perfected elsewhere,
it may be far more preferable, whenever possible, to make full use
of them through licensing agreements and use them as a springboard
for working out the techniques of a more advanced generation, thus
gaining time and, sometimes, money.

Other Fields

In 1965, the Medium-Term Economic Policy Committee (see
Chapter 4) set up a Scientific and Technological Research Work Group.
Its work made it possible for a Council of Ministers for Research
to meet in October 1967. This Council decided to undertake two
courses of action: to launch a collaboration in seven new fields

(dataprocessing, telecommunications, oceanography, and so forth); and to compare national programs.

The idea to set up an international collaboration was not a new one. For some years previous to this, similar attempts had been made, not only in the nuclear field but also in such other fields as space research, aeronautics, and certain basic research acitivities (high-energy physics and molecular biology). In 1971, for the countrie in the Community of Six, the total amount devoted to this collaboration amounted to 450 million ua, or about 9 percent of the total public research effort in the Community. *

But these collaborations, fruitful in basic research, were rather disappointing in such sectors as space research. The idea of widening this collaboration was flirted with in order to encompass new fields, but also in order to give it a firmer basis.

Where do we stand now with such a program? For the seven fields mentioned above, agreement has been reached on approximately 10 common courses of action. Thus, it has not all been for nought. Yet, the results are modest at best if one considers the sums at stake: about 40 million ua and one large-scale project—the European Weather Forecasting Center.

As for the bettering of conditions to promote research and innovation, discussions on a legal statute for the European company are still at a standstill; only those on the European patent have led anywhere. A comparison of the national programs did not start until early 1970 and is being carried on only very slowly: unquestionably, there has been an exchange of information between the different member countries' representatives, but no real comparison has taken place, and thus no assessment of their compatibility to any degree nor of their adequacy in the face of the needs of European society.

Thus, for research in general, as well as for the nuclear field (and this is also the case for space research), the accomplishments of Community or international collaboration have been modest indeed.

CONCLUSIONS

The causes of past disillusions, which have been analyzed many times, may be summed up under a few headings:

---

* In 1975, the Community's research and development expenditure amounted to 17 billion ua.

1. There has been no general underlying conception to orient research efforts.

2. Except for the nuclear field, the question has never been examined as to whether the fields chosen for international collaboration are those where this collaboration was likely to bring about highly beneficial results.

3. In nuclear matters, as in matters of space research, research projects have been undertaken without exactly knowing the goals and without foreseeing which industrial extension of these projects might give the results real value. International collaboration has often been undertaken in organizational conditions of extreme complexity and inefficiency.

4. Finally, the EEC members in general have shown their overriding interest in "fair returns," that is, each country expects to get back the equivalent or more of its financial contribution to the common project in the form of contracts granted to its laboratories or industries. If such a principle is applied, it is very difficult to entrust the project's accomplishment to the most effective teams.

These are the main reasons for the low level of effectiveness of international cooperation. However, we must go deeper into things if we want to offer solutions that have a chance of success.

First, this uncertainty over the research goals not only characterizes international projects but, until very recently, has been found at the national level as well: in the United States and in the USSR, it is primarily political and military motivations that have led their governments to intensify their research efforts, whereas in Europe, the governments have been driven by the desire to imitate and catch up with others. Only recently, after the disillusion experienced in the United States around 1968-69 over the apparently slight impact of research on the average citizen's life did European countries begin to set up the mechanisms for analyzing long-term needs and to select and organize research projects.

On the other hand, those taking part in collaboration efforts are not always convinced of the highly useful nature of the expected results. Governments aim, above all, at giving their scientists the best working conditions and their firms the best business prospects rather than at acquiring scientific knowledge or a technical end product (an apparatus or production process) that they may sorely need. Thus, a country will be interested in taking part in space research because it thinks it is the only way for it to set up research or production teams at the national level, which may then become independent of the Community effort.

It is not surprising, therefore, that countries want to have their outlay come back to their own territory, not so much in the form of financial investments but as work for their citizens, their laboratories, and their firms.

It was in full light of these various problems that the Commission formulated its organization proposals:

1. The first has as its purpose to set up an organization in charge of devising the Community's research policy, choosing orientations that will make it possible to meet Europe's foreseeable needs and, from these, to deduce which lines of research will need Community collaboration.

2. The second provides for a highly independent agency to be responsible for carrying out those projects that rank as Community projects.

In early 1973, the Commission set up the European Committee on Research and Development (ECRD), which was responsible for providing guidance in the choice of lines of research to undertake jointly.

In January 1974, the Council approved four resolutions concerning:

1. the coordination of national policies and the definition of activities of Community interest in technological science (for this, the Committee for Scientific and Technical Research (CSTR) was set up);

2. the participation of the European communities in the European Science Foundation;

3. a joint working program for the European communities in the field of science and technology; and

4. a working program for the European communities regarding forecasting, assessment, and methodology.

In October 1975, the Commission laid down the major guidelines of this Community policy by proposing two general directions to follow:

1. Research and development activities could be worked out in light of the policies pertaining to certain industries that the Community had retained in order to aid in the accomplishment of the objectives first set out in these policies (such as agriculture and the energy sector).

2. These older policies could be of use in defining new policies the Community wished to submit to discussion. To this end, the Commission suggested a certain number of sectors to be dealt with in priority in the following five years: natural resources (energy,

agriculture, and raw materials); the environment; economic and industrial development; and social conditions.

In the last analysis, what was it that we expected from the Common Market? We hoped to see an increase in trade, specialized production, and the opportunity for developing production on a scale that was only feasible against the background of a greatly expanded market. And what have we secured so far?

As far as trade is concerned, the increase has been spectacular. On the question of specialization, the answer must be more qualified— but positive. On the third point, however, the reply is still rather negative. The fields concerned are aircraft manufacture, dataprocessing, the building of nuclear power stations, space work, major apparatus for basic research, and a perfected mass production of various types of equipment for public services, such as urban transport. Of all these fields, aircraft production is the only one in which there has been any real effort that has borne fruit—in the Concorde and Airbus programs and an important regrouping of the firms concerned. In all the other fields, no appreciable progress has yet been achieved.

As things have turned out, the past results have been obtained in the traditional industries, for which the opening of the frontiers was a powerful stimulus to trade and, to a certain degree, to structural reorganization. In the newer industries, however, materially dependent as they are on public intervention (whether on public tenders or public aid for mitigating some of the special risks), there has been little progress due to lack of any agreement on a common policy to be followed in the fields concerned. It was not, in fact, until 1971 or 1972 that the first sectoral proposals for these fields made their appearance. The national attitudes vary from country to country, but they are all united in evading the main issues. Germany puts the accent on competition policy and the market economy as the instruments by which growth can be most quickly and best directed. France deems it necessary to strengthen her big firms at the national level before setting out on industrial reorganization at the Community level. The Netherlands rejects the idea of public intervention in industrial questions and would leave the big firms to be masters of their own destiny. Italy is mainly concerned with regional imbalances and thinks more of expanding the traditional industries than of encouraging those industries working on activities directed toward the future. These different attitudes have all played their part in delaying the possibility of concrete discussion on industrial policy.

NOTES

1. For a sectoral analysis of minimal sizes and the economies of scale, see C. F. Pratten, Economies of Scale in Manufacturing Industry (Cambridge: Cambridge University Press, 1971), or a condensed table in P. Maillet and John Pinder, "The Widening of the EEC as Seen from Both Sides of the English Channel," Revue d'Economie Politique (September 1972), p. 764.

2. Official Journal of the European Communities, May 30, 1967.

3. Communication de la Commission au Conseil du 23 juin 1971 (Official Journal of the European Communities, 4 November, 1971), p. 7.

4. For example, refer to: for Germany—Bericht des Bundeskartellamts über seine Tätigkeit i. J., 1970, vol. 28 (Bundestagsdrucksache VI/2380, June 1971), p. 34; for France—A. -P. Weber, Les concentrations industrielles dans la France Contemporaine (Paris-Montreal: Bordas, 1971), pp. 28, 43; for The Netherlands, Belgium, and the United States—H. W. De Jong, Ondernemingsconcentratie (Leiden: 1971), pp. 144, 145, 194.

5. Commission of the European Communities, Second Report on Competition Policy (April 1973).

6. Pratten, op. cit.

7. EEC Commission Memorandum on Community Policy in the Data-Processing Field (September 1975).

8. EEC Commission Memorandum on Action Program for the European Aircraft Industry (October 1975).

9. In this context, refer to the Protocol of April 21, 1964.

10. Refer to the EEC Commission, Third General Report (May 1960), p. 172.

11. See, for instance, the criticisms of Zeller and Garaudy in L'Imbroglio agricole du Marché Commun (Paris: Calmann-Levy, 1970)

12. EEC Commission, Report on Community Nuclear Policy, 1969.

The objectives concerning the effects of the Common Market
for the European are stated in the Preamble to the EEC Treaty,
where the member countries affirm "as the essential objective of
their efforts the constant improvement of the living and working
conditions of their peoples." They are also given in Article 2, which
speaks of an accelerated raising of the standard of living, and in
Article 117, which says:

> Member States agree upon the need to promote improved
> working conditions and an improved standard of living for
> workers, so as to make possible their harmonization
> while the improvement is being maintained.
> They believe that such a development will ensue
> not only from the functioning of the common market,
> which will favour the harmonization of social systems,
> but also from the procedures provided for in this
> Treaty and from the approximation of provisions laid
> down by law, regulation or administrative action.

The objectives laid down, then, are general goals rather than
precise objectives. It is the general forward movement of the Common Market that is counted on to attain these goals more than any
decisions made by the Community's public authorities. It is very
telling to notice that only an "approximation" of legal provisions and
regulations is spoken of and not a "harmonization," which would
necessarily mean unification. Here, in fact, it is a question of a
highly political domain, where 20 years ago, ideas varied from
country to country and where they may still evolve, depending on
changes of government. Thus, on one hand, the Treaty imagined

decisions being adopted in a limited number of cases where continued
disparities would seriously stand in the way of the working of the
Common Market and, on the other hand, a spontaneous movement
toward harmonization brought about both by more persons moving
between countries and by a greater knowledge of the accomplishments
of neighboring countries.

Purely Community action, then, has been in three main directions: bringing into force those harmonizations provided for in the
Treaty; providing a great deal of information regarding the comparisons between the different national systems of social security, workin
conditions, and so forth; and gradually working out a special common
conception of social policy.

Once again, even more than in the previous chapter, the lack
of precise objectives makes it impossible to assess to what degree
they have been attained. Thus, we are forced to treat the subject
in a less rigorous manner. Furthermore, it is interesting to see to
what degree the fears expressed at the time of the signing of the
Rome treaties have been realized:

1. Would not the use of the national product be increasingly
channeled into productive investment at the expense of social investment? In other words, would not the keener competition between
the different countries of the Community lead to excessive importance
being assigned to the growth rate, to the detriment (in the terminolog
used 15 years ago) of improvement in the forms of economic growth
or to the detriment of what would be called today the "quality of life"

2. Was there not a danger that the Common Market might be
an obstacle to bold social policies if countries desired to undertake
them, especially when it came to equalization of incomes and increasing the importance of income redistribution mechanisms?

3. Was there not a risk that the changes in production structur
arising from the opening of the borders would have a bad effect on
employment, both in general and for individual firms and regions?

Therefore, two main topics will be discussed here (leaving
employment problems to the next chapter): the raising of the standar
of living and improvement in living conditions; and income levels
and income redistribution.

IMPROVEMENT IN STANDARDS OF LIVING

A first indication of the improvement in the standard of living
is to be found in the real national product per capita. In the Community as a whole, it rose by about 95 percent between 1958 and 1974,
so that the annual increase was 4.5 percent.

If the figures are converted at the then-prevailing exchange rates, the average income in the Community in 1974 was no more than one-third lower than that in the United States, as opposed to about one-half lower 20 years earlier.

Between member countries, the gaps have markedly diminished, although Italy lags far behind. At the annual improvement rate, it would take about 30 years for Italy's average per capita GNP to reach the Community level. This gap is due primarily to the southern half of the country. *

It is, of course, impossible to state categorically that this improvement in standards of living is the direct consequence of the formation of the Common Market. There is, nevertheless, rather good circumstantial evidence to this effect, because of what has been said above about the increase in production. Furthermore the increase in trade has put a much larger range of goods at the disposal of the consumer.

TABLE 3.1

Evolution of GDP per Capita, EEC, 1960, 1970, and 1975
(EEC equals 100)

Country of Origin	1960	1970	1975	1975 (in ua)
Germany	113	124	132	5,150
France	113	113	121	4,730
Italy	60	70	60	2,330
Netherlands	83	99	114	4,440
Belgium	107	107	122	4,760
Luxembourg	141	127	116	4,540
United Kingdom	118	89	77	3,020
Ireland	55	54	49	1,900
Denmark	113	129	138	5,400
EEC	100	100	100	3,900

Source: SOEC.

---

* Income comparisons have been done on the basis of prevailing exchange rates, which is not a very satisfactory way of comparing the purchasing power of currency units. More valid comparisons must take into account the calculation of "shopping baskets of provisions" compared from one country to the next. Such a calculation was once made, in 1958, by the Statistical Office for ECSC workers. Unfortunately, it has never been remade, particularly on account

In the Community of Six, the trend has been toward a drawing closer together of the GDP per capita, except for Italy, which until around 1968 seemed to be catching up with the others, but then once again fell back in comparative terms. See Table 3.1.

Over the last 20 years, the United Kingdom has also been rather steadily and rapidly falling behind in relation to the others: the United Kingdom's recognition of this decline played a large part in pushing this country to join the Community.

No Community steps have been taken for the specific purpose of rechanneling in any special direction the resources that are available in increased quantities owing to the growth in production. But the fact holds true in all the countries that those areas where the increase in consumption has been the greatest are those where public assistance has been considerable.*

On several occasions in the last few years, public authorities have put forward the idea that the proportions of the GNP spent on public consumption and public amenities should increase faster than private consumption. This attitude is to be found both in national documents and in such Community documents as the First Medium-Term Policy Program. The latter document, however, takes no more than a general view; but some of the national documents, such as the French Plans, have given details and figures regarding the sectors to be given priority.

What has been the actual trend?

Between 1960 and 1970, the proportion of public consumption has shown an appreciable increase in Germany, Belgium, and The Netherlands, which contrasts with a decline in France. There has also been an increase in the proportion of public investments, which was very high in France and Belgium, as well as in Germany and The Netherlands.

The developments in the decade in question thus followed the course hoped for, but closer examination reveals that this was the case more particularly in the earlier part of the period. Between 1965 and 1970, with the Community GNP rising at the average rate

_____

of the noncomparability of increased retail prices in the various countries.

* This is primarily a matter of expenditure in health and education programs, where this contribution has reached 70 percent and 90 percent, respectively, as well as in public recreation, transp systems, and telecommunications, where the proportion of public allowances is sizable.

of 5.2 percent per annum, public consumption increased by 3.2 percent and public investment by 4.9 percent, compared with expectations of 4 percent and 8.5 percent. *

An explanation must therefore be sought for the fact that what was apparently considered to be a priority requirement, at any rate by a large part of the population, has not brought about a more substantial increase in the public expenditure devoted to satisfying these requirements.

An explanation is also needed for the large disparities between countries in the amount of public expenditures, particularly public investments. In this field, the disparity is so great that people have spoken of a Latin pattern and a Northern pattern.

The question is all the more pertinent since some commentators have put forward the idea that setting up the Common Market may have acted as a brake on growth in public expenditure, or, at the least, may have given the governments an alibi for not increasing it faster. The first argument is found in economic policy. In this connection, the increasingly open attitude toward the outside world and delays in the application of Community instruments have diminished the effectiveness of control through monetary investments; this may have led public authorities to fall back on budgetary methods of control, in which expenditure limitations have primarily cut into public investment.

This is a logical explanation, but its confirmation by the figures is only partial. The increase in investment by public administrations has indeed been halted, and there have even been cutbacks in Germany and Italy, but it has proceeded very regularly in France and fairly regularly in the Benelux countries. In the United Kingdom, too, there has been concurrently a very marked stop-and-go policy and a high level of public investment.

Another line of reasoning has it that the tax rate should not have been increased if each country was to remain equally competitive in relation to other member countries (an attitude shared by all the taxpayers) and that, above all, more public expenditure should have gone toward strengthening the economic infrastructure, which was to make the country more competitive, while postponing improvements in the social infrastructure (an attitude defended by the firms).

Regarding the overall level of expenditure, the size of the tax loads in Community countries has reached a level it would be difficult to exceed, both for sociological and political reasons. There would be a serious contradiction in the citizens' minds between their wish

---

* The years following were greatly disturbed by inflation and the energy crisis.

TABLE 3.2

Tax Load and Public Expenditure—Germany,
France, Italy, The Netherlands, and Belgium, 1958 and 1970
(percent of GNP)

Country of Origin	Tax Load		Consumption and Public Investments	
	1958	1970	1958	1970
Germany	22.4	23.9	17.1	20.1
France	22.9	21.6	15.7	15.5
Italy	17.5	18.4	15.1	15.2
Netherlands	21.9	25.5	20.8	21.1
Belgium	18.1	23.9	14.7	17.8

Source: SOEC.

for public amenities and their rejection of increased taxes. Furthermore, it can be seen in Table 3.2 that both for the tax load (the ratio
of taxes to GNP) and the ratio of public expenditure for consumption
and investment to GNP, the EEC countries fall into three groups: in
Germany and The Netherlands, this ratio attains its highest point;
in France and Italy, its lowest point; and in Belgium, it falls in between. It must also be mentioned that, except in France, over the
last 12 years, these ratios have been on the upswing, although there
has been no marked change in the position of the countries relative
to each other. This classification holds equally true for public expenditure.

Regarding the disparities between countries, three points are
to be noted.

1. Germany might be considered as having been, as of 1958,
particularly well prepared for the opening of borders and for its
entry into the Common Market. What we have seen above concerning
the compared development of trade tends to support this statement.
On the other hand, Italy, which was clearly lagging behind in the
industrialization process, should have made a special effort to push
ahead in industrialization upon its entry into the Common Market and
left aside public amenities, and, particularly, public amenities for
social aims. However, in The Netherlands, industrialization was
also lagging behind to a certain extent, a fact that led the Dutch gover-
ment to launch two industrialization plans after 1945. Although the
phenomenon was not as noticeable as in Italy, this industrialization
effort might have been expected to interfere with the development of
public amenities, particularly in a country so open toward the outside

Yet the experience shows that this has not been the case. Thus, the relative state of public amenities at the outset is not enough to explain the disparities in expenditure between the different countries.

2. In several countries, the distribution of tax revenue between the state and local authorities still remains rather close to the level of about a decade ago, whereas the balance should have tipped in favor of the local authorities as the prime contractors to meet the populations' needs. At the same time, the highest percentage of investments by public administrations has been recorded in the two countries that have most completely channeled large tax revenues to local authorities. Yet for the level of public investment and the level of urbanization, the classification is the same. Thus, the organization of the tax system may favor or handicap the financing of public amenities.

3. All the countries with a relatively low level of public investment—Italy, France, and Belgium—have two points in common: a tax system structure where direct taxes play a rather small part, as well as a marked hostility to taxes; and a much greater laxity toward tax evasion than exists in Northern countries.

We may wonder if the differences between countries do not reflect sociopolitical behavior more than economic policies. It is well-known that Latin peoples (in the EEC, the Italians) are more individualtstic than their Northern neighbors, new or old, in the Community. Likewise, in The Netherlands, the heritage of decentralized decision making accounts for the high level of investments by local authorities. This tendency for Community action may also stem from the everlasting need of the people living on the North Sea to dominate and tame their savage natural surroundings.

Also, the ideas of "collective needs" and "collective goods" are not clear-cut notions: only too often, the following three criteria are mixed:

1. the idea that some services can only come from equipment used by several persons at the same time and that this equipment must be publicly built and managed;

2. the idea that the responsibility for setting up and managing these services would belong to the public authorities when community needs are concerned—the real classification then depends on practices current in each country, the rationality of which we all know has neither been demonstrated nor even analyzed; and

3. the forms of financing: there would be collective needs when the public authorities take care of the financing on the basis of taxes.

Thus, the decisions to be made will take into consideration the scope of each kind of investment or expenditure, the way of financing (through taxes or prices), and the public or private responsibility for setting up the program and managing it.

The management of public funds to the best effect can only be had if needs are clearly defined and if distribution of authority between the public and private sector is boldly examined, including the form of financing used, whether by taxes or state fees. But there is no reason to start with why the choices should be the same in all the countries—even major regional disparities might be possible. Nor is a complete harmonization necessary. However, a common European sociopolitical and cultural framework will probably narrow the gaps. But an assessment of acceptable disparities can only be made with the help of relatively detailed studies. This assessment should become more feasible with the help of the PPBS procedures launched in every country and at the Community level.

INCOMES AND SOCIAL SECURITY

The Treaty of Rome called for "harmonization of living standard while improvement is being maintained." How far has the Community come on the problem of incomes in general, regional disparities, and social security systems?

Incomes

Has bringing the various economies into contact led to a standardization of pay conditions? (See Table 3.3.)

A brutal reply to this question is provided by two figures, which serve as examples: in 1970, on the basis of the exchange rates, the ratio of German figures to French figures was 0.98 for the GDP per industrial worker but as high as 1.67 for the direct hourly wage of the industrial male worker. This explains how one may note equivalent average standards of living in the two countries and yet note substantial disparities in hourly wages in two border regions, like Lorraine and the Saar or Alsace and Baden.

These disparities stem from the accumulated interplay of many factors, which are now going to be briefly surveyed.

In 1970, the ratio of per capita GNPs was 1.04. The ratio of the GDPs per person employed in the economy was already different, or 0.98 for France and Germany. * This is due to the fact that fewer

---

* This ratio of 0.98 covers up far greater disparities per secto It drops to 0.78 in agriculture and 0.91 in industry. On the other

TABLE 3.3

Comparison of Incomes and Pay in
Germany, France, Italy, The Netherlands, and Belgium, 1970
(100 = France)

Factors	Germany	France	Italy	Nether-lands	Belgium
GDP per capita	104	100	59	88	92
GDP per worker	98	100	67	95	96
Average salaried earnings	101	100	77	106	97
Annual direct wage	114	100	72	109	113
Annual direct wage in industry	126	100	79	114	110
Hourly direct wage in industry	138	100	88	120	119
Worker's hourly pay in industry	155	100	94	128	129
Hourly wage of male labor in industry	167	100	—	—	—

Source: SOEC and author's computations.

people were employed in France than in Germany. In The Netherlands, this percentage of employed is by far the lowest.

We may continue our analysis of wage rates for which comparable statistics are available.[*]

The overall wage per wage earner produced similar figures
in France and in Germany (a difference of one percent). The highest
figure is that for The Netherlands, although the GDP per active
population is slightly lower there than in France and Germany: this
means that wage-earning workers are relatively better paid in The
Netherlands than in the other countries, in comparison to the rest
of the active population. It is the same case in Italy, but for very
different reasons; in The Netherlands, it is the outcome of a deli-
berate wish for a certain income equality, whereas in Italy, it
results from a degree of overemployment in those activities where
the independent workers predominate (particularly agriculture).

___

hand, it rises to around 1 in services and much higher than 1 in the
civil service.

[*]In 1974, 80 percent of employment was salaried in the EEC of
Six and 83 percent in the EEC of Nine, as opposed to 90 percent in
the United States.

A basic distinction must be made between the direct wage of the wage earner and the overall wage, which includes the employers' contributions to social security and possible various benefits in kind. The overall wage distribution still is very different from one country to the next. In Italy, the percentage of indirect wages in the total is highest (43 percent), and in Germany, it is the lowest (31 percent). The markedly lower level in Germany as compared to France (40 percent) accounts for the fact that there is both an overall wage ratio of 1.01 and a ratio of direct wages and salaries (nonagricultural) as high as 1.13.

Sectoral wage disparities may also cause some overall gaps between countries. Thus, the industrial wages are relatively higher in Germany than in France. Likewise, the ratio Germany/France, which is 1.14 for nonagricultural wages as a whole, goes as high as 1.26 for industry, when taken alone.

The annual working period varies considerably from one country to the next. Even though the trend since setting up the Common Market has been to reduce the length of this working period, major structural differences between countries remain. For wage earners, this period is longest in France, and shortest in Italy.

The 8 percent difference between Germany and France accounts for the fact that, for direct wages, the ratio goes from 1.26 per year up to 1.38 per hour.

The length of the working period has an equalizing effect when it comes to yearly wages. This compensating phenomenon comes into play, particularly in the case of white collar workers.

Inequalities exist also in the wage rates between blue and white collar workers. The hourly cost of a white collar worker, though higher than that of a blue collar worker, is higher, with great variance—higher by 50 percent in Germany, by 60 percent in the Benelux countries, and by 90 percent in France and Italy. On the other hand, the proportion of employees in the total salaried industrial employment certainly tends to increase in all countries but still shows sizable disparities, ranging from 14 in Italy and 17 in Belgium to around 24 in the other countries. The ratio of hourly industrial wages between Germany and France goes from 138 for wage earners as a whole up to 155 for blue collar workers only.

Finally there is the part played by the difference between wages for men and those for women. Its effect is a complex one: (1) the size of the difference varies—smaller in France and Italy than in Germany, Belgium, and especially, The Netherlands; and (2) the proportion of female labor in industry is much smaller in The Netherlands than in the other countries. These differences between France and Germany explain why the ratio of the male worker's direct hourly

wage is 1.67, whereas the ratio of the direct hourly wage for industrial workers as a whole drops to 1.55. *

Thus, more than 10 years after the beginning of the Common
Market, wage structures still vary from country to country. One is
struck by the fact that, even if certain advances have been made in
equalizing wages, the special national characteristics are still very
much alive. National differences remain very strong, whether one
is speaking of the ratios of indirect wages to total wages, the
differences between the wages of blue and white collar workers or
the disparities between men's and women's wages. As a matter of
fact, France stands out as the nearest to an exception. The closeness in Dutch and Belgian behavior can be explained by the intensity
of both economic and cultural exchanges between these two countries.

Here, there is a contrast with what was earlier learned in
studying income spending. Whereas, with the latter, a certain
European behavior is forming, something that had been noted some
years ago,[1] in income distribution, the disparities remain sharper.
It may be that the forces acting to draw countries closer regarding
these two problems vary in nature and intensity. The standardization
of trade makes available a similar supply of goods to all Europeans,
and this encourages the forming of a uniform behavioral pattern. On
the other hand, income distribution results from the sociological and
political force ratios. Whether it is a question of (trade) unions or
political parties and their ideologies, the process of Europeanization
has remained very superficial: if European "federations" have been
formed, their major role still remains to increase the number of

---

* Comparing men's and women's wages also makes it possible
to see to what degree the objective set out in Article 119 of the
Treaty of Rome has been reached. Article 119 puts forward "the
principle that men and women should receive equal pay for equal
work." In all the countries, the drawing closer of man's and women's
wages can be observed.

It is true that the ratio of men's and women's wages (hourly
worker's earnings in industry) remains well below 1 (0.8 in France
and Italy, 0.7 in Germany and Belgium, and 0.6 in The Netherlands),
but in large part, this difference can be explained by the lower average
wage of female wage earners and, also, by the concentration of
women's jobs in branches of activity where wages fall below the average.

Thus, though it cannot be said that the goal of Article 119 has
been fully met (to make an accurate assessment of the situation, very
careful job comparisons would be needed), a clear advance toward
equality has nevertheless been made in all the countries, although
it is less marked in Germany and Belgium than elsewhere.

conventions, conferences, and the exchanges of information. The
setting up of a system of negotiation at the European level and the
launching of common operations stand out as exceptions. Wages
continue to be set by agreements at the national level, and the electo-
ral platforms of the political parties and the unions' demands continue to be dominated by problems that are of national interest. [*]

Regional Disequilibrium

Concerning regional problems, there was a fear expressed
when the Rome treaties were signed that the process of forming the
Common Market might essentially benefit that famous industrial
"triangle" which comprises the central regions of the Community
and that the so-called peripheral regions might expect to see their
situation deteriorate further, which was far from good in any case.
What has occurred since?
A first, or rather general, reply to this question may be given
by comparing the developments in five territorial groupings:

1. the industrial triangle—Lille-Amsterdam-Düsseldorf—which
is the home of one out of five inhabitants of the Community of Six;
2. a ring round this triangle in Germany and the Benelux
countries (10 percent of the population);
3. the Paris Basin and northwestern Italy (12 percent);[†]
4. the peripheral regions—western and southwestern France,
the eastern and southern regions of the Federal Republic of Germany,
and southern Italy (20 percent of the population); and
5. the rest of the Community, which is the home of a good
third of the population and comprises regions of various characters,
with the common characteristic that their population density and
degree of industrialization is below the average.

So far as the population is concerned, the relative changes
have been small. (See Table 3.4.) The most that can be noted is a
slight reduction in the peripheral regions and a rise in regions two
and three. On the other hand, the contribution made by each region
to the Community's GDP has undergone substantial changes. (See
Table 3.5.) These may be summarized as follows:

---

[*] The election of representatives to the European Parliament
by universal suffrage in 1978 may help to create political movements
of a "European" nature.
    [†] The first three areas comprise the "European crescent,"
which contains 43 percent of the population.

TABLE 3.4

Total Population of the Community of Six, 1954, 1960, and 1969

Area	1954	1960	1969
Northwest Europe in the strictest sense	19.6	19.7	19.6
Northwest Europe in the largest sense	29.2	29.5	30.1
Northwest Europe in the largest sense, Paris basin and northwest Italy	40.8	41.8	42.9
Peripheral areas	22.7	21.7	21.1
Rest of the Community	36.5	36.5	36.0

TABLE 3.5

Comparative Share in the Community GDP, 1960 and 1969

Area	1960	1969
Northwest Europe in the strictest sense	26.0	25.0
Northwest Europe in the largest sense	37.0	41.0
Northwest Europe in the largest sense, Paris basin, and northwest Italy	52.0	57.0
Peripheral areas	16.5	16.0
Rest of the Community	31.5	27.0

TABLE 3.6

Evolution of the GDP per Capita in Relation
to the Community Average, 1957 and 1969
(= 100)

Area	1957	1969
Northwest Europe in the strictest sense	124	114
Northwest Europe in the largest sense	117	115
Northwest Europe in the largest sense, Paris basin, and northwest Italy	115	115
Peripheral areas	75	76

1. The share of the industrial triangle seems to be slightly declining. In particular, the share of North Rhine-Westphalia has fallen appreciably.

2. The share of the peripheral regions is practically unchanged

3. The share of the ring around the industrial triangle is increasing very substantially, having risen from 11 percent to 16 percent of the total.

4. Neither the Paris Basin nor northwestern Italy shows any change in their comparative positions.

5. The comparative share of the rest is suffering a decrease.

In per capita production, the industrial triangle is losing a part of its lead, but the relative backwardness of the peripheral regions remains as it was. (See Table 3.6.)

The general impression is that, during the first 12 years, there was little change in the comparative position of the old industrial regions and the peripheral regions. In the peripheral regions, regional measures, which successfully prevented backwardness from growing worse, were not able to cancel it out or even lessen it. As for the old industrial regions, they did not profit from the Common Market's formation, probably because their industries were slow-growth or even declining industries; the new industries established themselves on the fringe of this triangle, which was already very populous, choosing those areas that offered the greatest flexibility in which to establish themselves.

Italy's case deserves special consideration here, given the extreme differences between the conditions in the country's north and south. In Lombardy, the per capita GNP is very close to the Community level. In the north and center combined, where two-thirds of the population is to be found, it is only 20 percent below this level, whereas in the south, it only reaches 45 percent of the Community level, a gap that has not been narrowed appreciably over the last 15 years. Unemployment was still at 4 percent to 4.5 percent in 1969, against the national average of 2.7 percent and less than 2 percent in Lombardy and Piedmont. The comparative position has not improved, even though, between 1951 and 1971, more than 4 million people left the Mezzogiorno (South Italy) to settle in other regions of Italy or the Community.

At the regional level, in effect, everything occurs as if the measures used by the public authorities to fight against the regional imbalances had successfully held them down, but in fact, these measures have not even managed to reduce the disparities or provid a sufficient boost to backward regions to enable them to narrow the gap between them and the rest of the territory. For this reason, the disparities in living standards between different regions still remain very large:

thus, the gross product per capita is around four or five times greater in Hamburg and in the Paris area than in the poorest areas of the Community (west Ireland and southern Italy). (See Table 3.7.)

TABLE 3.7

Gross Product Distribution of Germany, France, Italy
The Netherlands, Belgium, and the United Kingdom
(national level = 100)

Country	Distribution
Germany (11 Länder)	161/81
France (21 regions)	148/71
Italy (20 regions)	136/52
Netherlands (11 provinces)	119/76
Belgium (9 provinces)	119/72
United Kingdom (11 regions)	115/82

Source: SOEC regional statistics.

For a long time, almost all measures have been national ones, and Community intervention has been very restricted in scope.

The Treaty of Rome says little of this question. Regional problems are spoken of in only two places: in Article 92, concerning state-granted subsidies (discussed in Chapter 2); and in Articles 129 and 130, concerning the European Investment Bank (EIB).

It must be added that Article 56 of the ECSC Treaty makes possible the financing of programs to establish new activities that are likely to ensure the productive re-employment of the labor force that will be available due to a decline in regional employment in the steel and coal industries.

Thus, at the beginning, Community action took the following forms: (1) starting up major studies in regions hit by developments in the mining and steel industries; (2) overseeing the aids and subsidies granted by the states and making an effort to prevent over-bidding between national aids, which results in waste and which is likely to benefit outside countries; and (3) well-timed actions, thanks to the ECSC provisions, the Social Fund, and the European Investment Bank. (These will be described in a later section.)

On July 25, 1973, the Commission proposed that a European Regional Development fund be set up, which would make a Community contribution possible. This, to be effective, would have to "meet three criteria: it must be complementary to but not replace national regional policies, have operating flexibility, and grant aid insofar

as assisted investments were part of development programs or
corresponded to regional development objectives." Several years
of preparatory talks went into this proposal, which was adopted in
December 1974 by the Paris Summit Conference, which decided to
set up a European Regional Development Fund (ERDF), backed by the
Community's own financial resources. Point Five of the Final Paris
Summit communique stated that this ERDF

> whose intervention, coordinated with national regional
> aids, will make it possible, along with the gradual
> realization of economic and monetary union, to correct
> the main regional imbalances within the enlarged Com-
> munity, particularly those resulting from a predominance
> of agriculture, industrial change and structural under-
> employment.

Although this general idea of solidarity in favor of problem
regions was thus recognized, it was still necessary to clarify it in
its application. In fact, two general approaches are conceivable.
In one, the whole Community is considered—the individual countries
are disregarded—on the basis of various objective indicators (the
unemployment rate, average income levels, and so forth), and the
regions most in need of aid are defined. In the other, the same
objective criteria are taken into consideration, but they are applied
within the territory of each country.
It is obvious that, in the Community as it is right now, these
two approaches yield entirely different priority regions: with the
first, we come up with much of Italy and Ireland and very little of
other countries' territory. This latter territory would increase
sharply with the second approach, and thus with the same amount
from the ERDF, Italy's and Ireland's share would be smaller. If
one takes national aids into account as well, it may be said that the
ERDF's resources must be put to use, first, in those countries that
already grant substantial aids, since, in this, they have proved they
attach great importance to correcting regional imbalances—or, con-
trarily, first put them to use in the other countries, to offset the
disparities between national policies. Here, it can be seen how
blurred the idea of solidarity is.
For 1975, the ERDF was allocated 300 million ua and 500
million ua for the year following. Although not negligible, these
remain very modest sums (0.05 percent of the Community product).
The proportion to which each country was entitled was set at the
outset: the ERDF will, thus, essentially favor Italy, the United
Kingdom, and Ireland. Yet the principle was laid down that these
aids should not replace national ones but act to buttress them.

Social Security

The concept of harmonization of social security systems,
which is discussed in Article 117 of the Treaty of Rome, is not self-
explanatory. It is important, in the first place, to agree on the
meaning of "harmonization," which is named as one of the effects
expected from the operation of the Common Market.

In 1958, overall similarities manifested themselves between
the countries side by side with dissimilarities of detail. The total
amount of redistribution expenditure represented sums varying
between 10.6 percent and 14.1 percent of the GNP. In overall terms,
therefore, there were no considerable gaps that might, in themselves,
have hindered the establishment of an economic balance in the Community. This overall closeness in the percentages explains why one
problem was never really raised: was it necessary to standardize
social security systems to facilitate the working of the Common
Market? (This is a question over which theoreticians are divided.)
It would have come fully to the surface with the United Kingdom's
entry into the Common Market had not this country decided to over-
haul its social security financing mechanism.

However, there were great differences in the functional distribution of social expenditure. (See Figure 3.1.) In 1962, for example, Germany was giving a great deal less in family benefits than was France,
but materially more in old age, death, and survivor benefits. These
sizable differences were the result of different national habits. The positions have changed considerably since then, and the disparities are
smaller.

Social expenditure in all the countries has taken on increasing
importance in relation to GNP, and in real value. Thus, it is possible
to speak of a harmonization while improvement is being maintained,
since the disparity between social expenditure (in percentage of
GNP) has been lessened in the course of a general increase. The
ratio of social expenditure per capita in the two extreme cases,
Germany and Italy, has thus dropped from 2.3 to 1.9.

At the same time, a de facto harmonization has occurred in
the distribution of social expenditure—for example, a comparative
drop in dependents' allowances in France but an increase in Germany
and Italy—whereas there was an increase in state health insurance
everywhere, but this increase was greatest in Belgium, which started
at the lowest level. The harmonization effect was not systematically
sought but came about due to the converging of different national
ideas, which, in turn, was the result of a constant mutual exchange
of information aimed for and developed by the Commission and its
social partners.

This drawing closer does not mean absolute standardization;
between Community countries, differences continue to exist for the

FIGURE 3.1

Functional Distribution of Social Expenditure

	Germany 1962	Germany 1973	France 1962	France 1973	Italy 1962	Italy 1973	The Netherlands 1962	The Netherlands 1973	Belgium 1962	Belgium 1973	U.K. 1973	Ireland 1973	Denmark 1973
Miscellaneous	16	9	16	8	17	12	12	5	22	17	7	7	6
Old Age	47	45	32	41	33	35	46	38	40	39	49	36	32
Health Insurance	30	37	22	31	26	44	28	45	18	28	35	39	46
Dependents' Allowances (Minors)	7	9	30	20	24	9	14	12	20	16	9	18	16

Source: SOEC.

86

proportion of the population that has health and maternity coverage, and there are real differences regarding the number of children covered by family allowances (with percentages found in France and the Benelux countries). [2]

Does this development promote or hinder the free movement of goods and persons?

As for goods and (therefore) production costs alone, it was observed that the disparities were greater for direct wages than for overall wages, that is, the cost of labor for the firm. Thus, for an industry whose products were particularly suited for trade, in 1970, between two extreme countries, Germany and Italy, a total wage costs ratio of 1.4 was recorded, as opposed to a direct wage ratio of 1.6. Here is a difference that theory, in some ways, can account for perfectly: for two countries with free trade between them, the exchange rate (which we have used in order to bring the available figures, which are given in national currencies, into a common unit) tends to find its level, so that production costs in the two countries are close. However, splitting up the total labor charges between the various elements is left to the discretion of each country, with the opening of the borders for goods in no way cutting into this freedom of decision.

It might turn out differently regarding the freedom of movement for workers, who may show a preference for one system of distribution between direct and indirect pay over another. Actually, professional migrations between countries by nationals of the six member states have been small. Thus, it has not been necessary to seek to standardize social security systems. On the other hand, it has been necessary to deal with the different national arrangements for migrant workers and their families. Regulations have been made regarding this in order to adapt these arrangements to the necessities of the free movement of workers, since these arrangements as established in national laws might have constituted an obstacle to the movements of labor or discriminated against Community workers from other countries in favor of home nationals.

In conclusion, it is interesting to notice the new concept of "harmonization" that developed as the Common Market came into existence. The new concept is one of seeking to equalize at a higher overall level than before. Here, the results obtained are a positive factor for a better European integration. They demonstrate as well that the Commission's setting up of a system of continuous documentation, its organizing exchanges of ideas, and the making of recommendations may have had a beneficial effect.

From what has preceded, two conclusions may be drawn: one concerning the relative success of the Treaty's objectives and the other the working of certain economic mechanisms.

First of all, it must be noted that great disparities continue to exist in income structure. Although there has been some "approximation" for earned incomes, the distribution between direct and indirect pay, the relative levels between large industrial sectors, and the ratio of men's pay to women's pay still vary greatly from country to country. The harmonization of social systems, taken in their largest sense, has been comparatively small.

However, at the same time, it must be noted that, despite some forecasts, these disparities have not brought about large labor migrations between countries; the biggest movements seem to center around the borders. The differences in the living conditions necessary to generate these relocations go far beyond the mere direct pay of the wage earner—so much so, in fact, that, in the aggregate, the notion of living standards has been enlarged beyond the mere quantitative aspects to consider the "quality of life." Similarly, the unions are discovering in the face of wildcat strikes that the limited aspect of pay rates and the length of the work week is no longer the crucial thing in their basic demands. Working conditions in the factory and living conditions in the city are taking on more and more importance, and in choosing his place of work (to the extent that a choice is really possible), the individual looks at his living and working conditions from a much broader standpoint than before.

In Chapter 6, therefore, the question of how much "approximation" of the legal, regulatory, and administrative procedures and practices is really necessary will be raised again.

NOTES

1. See André Piatier, Structure et perspectives de la Consommation européenne (Paris: 1967).

2. EEC Commission, Report on the Development of the Social Situation in the Community, Annual publication.

CHAPTER

4

MACROECONOMIC
ADJUSTMENTS

The style of the Treaty of Rome varies markedly, depending
on the subject. In the part entitled "The Foundations of the Community," where the four freedoms (the free movement of goods, persons,
services, and capital), as well as two common policies—for agriculture and transport—are to be found, everything is very exactly
stated, often with a precise calender to be followed.

On the other hand, in the third part, entitled "Policy of the
Community," where economic policy and the balance of payments
are dealt with, the terminology becomes looser: no longer is it a
question of the imperatives met previously (the states shall refrain,
shall abolish, shall modify, and so on); no longer is a timetable
spoken of. In Title II, "Economic Policy," the states regard their
economic policies as a matter of common concern. They consult
each other, and if the Council decides upon measures, it is by
acting unanimously. And last, there is not a word about growth
policy.

Why are there such overwhelming differences? At the time
of signing the treaties, there was a general consensus that the free
movement of goods and production factors could provide a stimulus
to efficient production. In the closely partitioned postwar world,
abolishing obstacles at the borders seemed the crucial task. Yet,
the experts disagreed when it came to deciding to what degree tax
systems, regulations, legal provisions, and social systems should
be harmonized. The principle of these harmonizations was thus
hidden away in the third part of the Treaty, formulated in flexible
and careful language. When it came to macroeconomic policy,
the states disagreed considerably. Over growth policy, the main
split—at least verbally—was between France, which had its own
planning commission and four-year plan, and Germany, which

supported a social market economy (see below). This split was so profound that the question of whether a growth policy might be led by the public authority was completely skirted.

However, it was impossible to ignore the question of economic policy, though here, too, there were great differences of opinion. Of course, the terms balanced expansion and increased stability used in Article 2 of the Treaty have been interpreted in all the countries as implying the maintenance of full employment and stable prices in a general expansion movement. The equilibrium in the balance of payments is everywhere recognized as a necessary condition for accomplishing these objectives, but it is far from sufficient in itself. But attitudes differ from country to country as to which objective comes first (with France accepting, like it or not, a rise in prices much higher than what Germany will accept.) There was no less divergence over the means to be employed to ensure "expansion i stable conditions": thus, Germany and Italy turned exclusively to monetary instruments, whereas France used a wide range of instruments, including price controls. If one adds that the member states had no intention of losing their autonomy in this matter, the only compromise option left was to provide for consultations—and, in some cases, decisions by unanimous vote. The result was the following passages:

Article 103

1. Member States shall regard their conjunctural [economic] policies as a matter of common concern. They shall consult each other and the Commission on the measures to be taken in the light of the prevailing circumstances.

Article 104

Each member State shall pursue the economic policy needed to ensur the equilibrium of its overall balance of payments and to maintain confidence in its currency, while taking care to ensure a high level of employment and a stable level of prices.

Article 105

1. In order to facilitate attainment of the objectives set out in Article 104, Member States shall coordinate their economic policies They shall for this purpose provide for cooperation between their appropriate administrative departments and between their central banks.

The Commission shall submit to the Council recommendations on how to achieve such cooperation.

Article 107

1. Each Member State shall treat its policy with regard to rates of exchange as a matter of common concern.

It is striking how carefully worded these sections are. In particular, the definition of the "measures appropriate to the working of the Common Market" is left to the discretion of the Treaty's executors.

Thus, these problems will be treated under the following four headings:

1. growth policy;
2. theoretical aspects of economic adjustment and monetary policy;
3. economic policy at work; and
4. the progress made on the road to monetary union.

MEDIUM-TERM PLANNING

Nowhere does the Treaty mention the possibility of a growth policy that would fall under the jurisdication of the public authority. It relies primarily on market mechanisms, on a strengthened competition coming from the opening of the borders and an active alertness on the part of the Community institutions, on the movements of the factors of production, and, particularly, on the spontaneous redirection of capital toward the most productive uses. It is only to make easier the vocational relocation of labor and to mitigate regional imbalances that the Treaty explicitly mentions measures to be taken, on the Community level in the first case and on the national level (under Community supervision) in the second.

As mentioned previously, this position is the outcome of a compromise between very different conceptions of economic policy on the part of the signers of the Treaty. It may also be explained by the fact that, around 1956-57, the mechanisms of economic growth had not yet been analyzed to the degree they have been today.

During the first years of the Community, all efforts went into eliminating obstacles to trade and the national differences that might most interfere with the working of a real common market. There was no attempt made to directly influence growth. It seemed all the less necessary since all the EEC countries were experiencing a high rate of growth; even Belgium, which trailed the leaders, underwent considerable expansion.

However, the fact could not be long overlooked that the public authority was expecting a substantial influence on the growth process, even if this influence took very different forms from one country to another.

The differences in the states of mind between France and Germany were particularly perceptible.

In Germany, confidence was placed in the behavior of economic agents acting in a decentralized way to ensure the most rapid growth. The underlying economic foundation for such an approach is twofold: it is a question of the guiding role of prices and the motor role of personal interest. The state's role is therefore to ensure through its legal mechanisms that this competition and these markets work as smoothly as possible, while the economy's vitality is to be ensured by the sum total of every individual's drive, where each person, submitted to the competition of others, will always try to do better to ensure his survival and success.

This conception does not rule out state intervention, namely, putting the GNP to use for certain ends, for example, hospitals and so forth. However, it does rule out interventions in favor of any particular sector of activity. Such is the general theoretical profile of the German conception, which is derived to a large extent from the works of the Freiburg school and the theoreticians of the Soziale Marktwirtschaft (social market economy).

In France, the "Plan" is not a substitute for the market, but a necessary complement to the extent that the market does not suffice to create long-term economic indicators. The Plan also acts as an "uncertainty reducing agent" (but it leaves a second basic role to the market, which is to sanction the decisions made by firms). Finally, putting the Plan into action is to be made easier by government intervention in various fields.

Two major differences come out of this divergence of attitude: (1) the German government long resisted the idea of having its government departments work out official medium-term forecasts that were meant to be made public; and (2) whereas the planned economy had been set up as a system in France, in Germany, the idea of institutional planning had long been looked upon with disfavor. In the rest of the Community, the attitudes fell somewhere between these two.

In The Netherlands, a public organization has existed since 1945, called the Centraal Planbureau. The basic activity of this bureau consists in preparing an annual "plan." Until very recently, The Netherlands did not have a medium-term plan covering the whole economy. However, for about 12 years, more than ever before, the government has stressed the objective of economic growth.

In Belgium, in 1959, a Bureau of Economic Planning was set up. Its role was similar to that of the Commissariat au Plan in France and its working methods are very similar, particularly regarding talks with business leaders in the various industries, but it has not taken on the same importance in the national economic life.

In Italy, after the Second World War, the general economic theory in force looked favorably on the market mechanism and the decentralization of economic decisions. Thus, the state thought it necessary to concentrate its efforts on maintaining monetary stability and some specific and carefully limited interventions.

Only with the "schéma Vanoni," formulated in 1954, did a description of economic mechanisms come to the fore that would have made possible, over a ten-year period, a reduction in unemployment and regional imbalances. Yet, Italy is still a long way from having any general plan.

It was a document presented by Minister La Malfa in 1962 that led to the setting up of a National Economic Planning Commission, which was to "lay out the guidelines of economic development plan for the country." In fact, changes in the unstable political situation cut off this commission's work before it was finished. In 1965, it was replaced by a Planning Bureau, which has not yet managed to play an important role in the economic life of the country.

In the early 1960s, the United Kingdom attempted an experiment in medium-term planning, which also drew on the French experiment, by setting up the National Economic Development Council. But the experiment came to nothing.

But even if the economic philosophy and administrative organization were different in each country, public intervention was a general phenomenon. Public contribution to the investment financing is a particularly clear example of this: except for Belgium, in all the countries, the "gross savings" of the public administrations (the difference between the tax revenue and operating expenses) exceeds the amount of public investments, and this difference is much higher in Germany than in France.

Would it therefore be possible to let each country define its own medium-term economic policy independently of the courses followed by the others, to be limited only by the rules of the Treaty? Three different kinds of reasoning all yield a negative answer:

1. The interpenetration of economies alters the range of possible developments for each country.

2. The compatibility that is important for the chosen ends is equally important for the means used; thus, the means considered by one country must be examined to see that they neither interfere with nor contradict those used by another.

3. It must not be forgotten that European construction is not only—or even mainly—economic in nature: the goal is political union. Thus, it is important that Europeans work out together what kind of society they want.

Aware of these considerations, especially the first two, the Commission quickly felt the need to institutionalize the instructions laid out in Articles 6 and 145 of the Treaty: "The Member States, in close cooperation with the Community's institutions, will coordinate their general economic policies to ensure that the objectives set out in this Treaty are attained." To this end, in 1963, the Commissic sent the Council a recommendation, which was followed on April 15, 1964, by the setting up of a Committee for Medium-Term Economic Policy, whose

> task is to draw on all the available information and
> particularly on those studies planned by a group of
> experts working with the Commission and from this to
> prepare a preliminary draft of a Medium-term Economic
> Policy Program. It will also lay out the general framework
> of the economic policies which the Member States and
> the Community Institutions propose to follow during the
> period under consideration and to ensure the coordination
> of these policies. This Program will cover a five-year
> period. On the basis of work done by the Committee
> for Medium-Term Economic Policy, the Commission
> will draft a preliminary Program. This preliminary
> Program will mention the points where it diverges
> from the Committee's preliminary draft.

Up until now, the Committee for Medium-Term Economic Policy has prepared four programs that have been adopted by the Council.[*]

The first program, adopted on April 11, 1967, applied to the period 1966-70.

It contains, following the introduction, a chapter that lays out the general conception of medium-term economic policy. The first chapter is followed by an analysis of the general conditions for economic growth over the next few years, an analysis that traces the general projections for medium-term economic development.

Then, the program lays out the first general guidelines regardi the various fields of medium-term economic policy. The employmen and vocation-training policies, public finance, and regional policy are dealt with more completely in the chapters following.

The second program, adopted on May 12, 1969, deals with the same period. Actually, it is a continuation and expansion in depth

---

[*] In 1974, this committee was grouped together with the Budget and Conjunctural Policy committees to form one big Economic Polic Committee.

of the first, especially as regards structural adaptation of firms and industries, agricultural policy, scientific and technical research, saving and investment financing, and economic policy. The two first programs together thus cover most medium-term development problems, except for those concerning international relations.

The third program, adopted on February 9, 1971, is very different in style. Its central theme is "the balanced development of the Community." Dealing with the prospects of economic and monetary union, it centers on problems of price stability and the protection of the external equilibrium.

Whereas the first three programs had been worked out in conditions of worldwide economic expansion and great European economic growth, the fourth program was drawn up in a Community directly hit by the recession. Therefore, it took up positions on a number of basic problems facing the economic leaders of all the countries:

1. Priority was given to a lasting return to full employment, for which price stability and growth were the basic conditions necessary; by 1980 at the latest, the rate of inflation was to be cut to 4 percent or 5 percent and the return to full employment assured.

2. On the growth problem, the position taken was clear: only sustained growth could make it possible to find solutions to the many current problems; an annual average growth rate in GDP of 4.5 percent to 5 percent was needed (slightly more in France and a little less in the United Kingdom).

3. The external trade balance was to show a surplus by 1980 (of around 0.5 percent to 1 percent of the GDP).

These objectives can only be attained through a stricter discipline in monetary policy and public finances, an intense investment effort, better coordination of the Community's internal policies, and by making more dynamic use of the Community's weight in the world.

It is very difficult to pass judgment on these experiments in Community planning. In fact, a line should be drawn between what was written in the texts and the actual procedures followed.

In the texts themselves, one is struck by the very general way things are expressed; in large part, they are quite removed from time and space. The figures only concern the large macroeconomic indicators. Thus, no basic information should be sought in these documents from which to work out partial studies (as might be done from the French plan) nor should one try to verify the compability of the projections or the national programs. (At best, attempts were made to see if the various national hypotheses on intra-Community trade were not incompatible in overall terms.) As far as the means go, there are a multitude of options, but it is just that which robs them of much of their usefulness, since there has been neither any position taken on the effectiveness of the means to be used nor any list of priorities drawn up on the means to be used first. In a word, it is hardly possible to sketch a panorama of the European society of tomorrow on this basis.

It is tempting to look on these documents, therefore, a little as school projects, albeit of high intellectual stature; the European Parliament has often expressed its disappointment that these texts were not more concrete.

However, such an approach would only give us half the picture and leave out a fundamental point—the fact that drawing up these documents served to teach those who took part in the drafting. As with the other Community committees, the meetings of the Medium-Term Economic Policy Committee helped its members to better know and understand the positions of the different EEC members and to grasp in what way these positions were linked to each country's own internal situation and to what degree they were generally valid. Along this line, for example, the Germans gradually discovered that French-style planning was not the diabolical instrument they had often thought it to be, and the French, on the other hand, became aware of the part played by competition in increasing productivity. Similarly, France's participation in the Brussels meetings helped the French to better set French economic development in a larger context—that of the Community and the world at large. Likewise, the Brussels debates probably influenced those articles in the German stabilization law of 1967 that provided for the yearly drafting of five-year estimates of public expenditure.

We would have to peer into men's hearts and heads to determine the real scope of these contacts. In 1969, in a memorandum on the progress of the first program, the Commission wrote:

> Halfway through the first Program, it appears that
> concerns over its implementation have only been
> slightly justified by the facts, possibly due to a cer-
> tain optimism on the Committee's part when drafting
> its Program, but also because of an incomplete adapta-
> tion of certain national measures to accept ideas agreed
> upon in common by the Member States. Above all,
> this is due to the fact that the Community's decision-
> making procedures and structures are inadequate to the
> tasks to be fulfilled. There has been some difficulty in
> ensuring that the different sectors draw closer in a
> consistent fashion to the goals set out at the beginning
> and with which they are supposed to fall in line.

This is a profound diagnosis: because of the very general for-
mulation of the medium-term program, it needed—and still needs—to
be given reality in true programs of action, either at the national
or Community level. Moreover, the official text reads: "The Council of the European Communities and the governments of the Member
States herewith adopt the nth Medium-Term Economic Policy Program
below and agree to follow the guidelines laid out herein."

At the national level, each country may give whatever meaning
it wants to these very general "guidelines." At the Community level,
the program is not yet the text wherein inspiration may be found for
making definite first steps. Whenever the program is referred to in
various Community documents, it is more out of courtesy than anything else.

It is the same case for forecasting studies on energy or agriculture, as well as some industrial sectors. Similarly, medium-
term budget estimates (five years) worked out each year since 1971
certainly make use of the overall growth hypotheses of the Medium-
Term Economic Policy Program but cannot find in it any elements
that provide for the different items of expenditure.

Such a state of affairs is much to be regretted. Here, everyone avoids making use of the very instrument that would make it
possible to ensure that the various ventures undertaken and the various
actions launched would be consistent.

ECONOMIC CONTROL AND MONETARY POLICY

In order to understand and evaluate the effects of the Common
Market in this field, it would be a good thing to review the underlying
theory, specifying the nature of the problems to be resolved and
presenting the various possible solutions. Only after that can one
adequately assess the scope of the measures that have already been
taken and explain why there has been relatively little progress in this
field.

There are two avenues of approach to the problem: Does the
interpenetration of economies change the facts of the problem? Does
a good working of the Common Market require any special developments?

The Common Market and Economic Stability

What effects on economic stability may one expect from an
increase in trade within the EEC?

For any determined country, the existence of sizable foreign
trade, with due allowance for the GNP, may maintain growth even

when demand drops if the economic conditions in the neighboring
countries remain good. On the other hand, turning to increased
imports in boom conditions is likely to reduce demand pull—often
inflationary—on the home market: but these favorable effects can
only come about if the external and external business cycles are out
of phase. If this is not the case, unfavorable results may arise from
an increase in trade: for instance, a weakening in exports may be
added to a sag in internal demand.

A skeletal model makes it possible to get a first quantitative
idea of the effects of a trade intensification between two countries of
similar size whose internal demand business cycles develop differentl
If, into this oversimplified model, we introduce as a value of growth
in bilateral trade that recorded for Germany-France between 1958
and 1970, we note that such trade intensification only reduces the
fluctuations in the domestic product by around 2 percent, if the business cycles in the two countries are not correlated, and by around 4
percent, if their movements are dramatically opposed. [*] Contrary to
what might first be thought, a complete parallelism in business cycle
does not mean an intensification of fluctuations at the national level:
the size of these fluctuations will quite simply remain unchanged. [†]

Since, in the case of the Common Market, one country's trade
intensification affects its relations with its five partners, the moderation of fluctuations in output may be greater: under especially
favorable conditions, for any determined country (with the economic
movement being exactly the opposite in all the other member countries), the theoretical result may reach around 10 percent, which
means that a fluctuation margin of 95-105 is reduced to 95.5-104.5. [*]

Comparing the size of economic fluctuations for the periods
1951-58 and 1959-71 shows a great decrease for Belgium and The
Netherlands and a much smaller decrease for France. However, for
Germany, no change is observed, and for Italy, especially, the
phenomenon takes the opposite course. Therefore, the results are
consistent with the conclusions of the model previously sketched for
Belgium, The Netherlands, and France but not for Germany and
Italy.

---

[*] These percentages apply to the fluctuations themselves, that
is, a fluctuation of the GNP between 95 and 105 would be brought dow
in the second case, to a fluctuation of between 95.2 and 104.8.

[†] This does not mean that a drawing closer of the curves of
the business cycles does not intensify the fluctuations: if the correlat
goes from -1 to +1, these fluctuations increase, in the given model,
by 6 percent.

[**] The theoretical case deals with countries of comparable
size when the share of trade in the GNP is moderate. (The last

As a matter of fact, other factors act to strengthen or counteract this mechanical effect. (See Table 4.1.)

First of all, some products are more affected by business cycles
than others, and trade structures can thus play an important role.
Thus, the figures for 1959 and 1970 display a great difference between
countries. This may account for the fact that the size of the fluctuation is more marked in Germany than in The Netherlands. Moreover,
whereas the product breakdown between the two groups changes
slightly for the other countries, the proportion of sensitive products
rises greatly in Italy; therein may lie an explanation, at least in part,
for the increase in economic fluctuations in this country.

On the other hand, the previous model was based on an unchanged
balance of foreign trade, whereas with changes in business cycles,
this may act as a stabilizing or destabilizing factor: an increase in
the balance (export-import) in sluggish economic conditions will be to
the advantage of the economy of the country in question; its effect
on other countries' economies will be beneficial if these economies
are in a boom cycle, but harmful in the contrary case. An analysis
of the 1960-70 decade brings three facts to light:

1. Germany, France, and Italy experienced a reduction in their
intra-Community trade balance (goods and services) in almost all
periods of rapid growth and an increase when there was a small rise
or drop in internal demand. These countries, therefore, exported
their boom and slump conditions, with a side effect of a reduction of
the fluctuations in their national output.

2. In Belgium and The Netherlands, the reverse was true, that
is, there was an increase in the balance in a rapid growth period,
and a drop when there was a slowdown in expansion.

3. Because economies were out of phase with each other to a
certain degree during 1959-70, there was a series of cases of auto-
matic mutual support that helped boost the growth of those member
countries going through a sluggish period.*

Also the psychological factors must not be forgotten: entrepreneurs who are experiencing sluggish conditions at home and who
see the investments of their foreign competitors continue to increase
(due to better economic conditions) might keep up the level of their
own investments so that they will later be in a situation to face the
competition.

---

hypothesis makes it possible to speak of an autonomous internal
business cycle.) Thus, it is applicable neither to the Benelux countries nor to relations with the United States.

* Since 1973, the situations are more in phase in all countries.

TABLE 4.1

Breakdown of Intra-Community Exports by Their Sensitivity to Economic Cycles, 1959 and 1970
(percent)

Country of Origin	Class 1[a] (Rather Sensitive Products)		Class 2[b] (Not Very Sensitive Products)		Total
	1959	1970	1959	1970	
Germany	78	72	22	28	100
France	60	55	40	45	100
Italy	33	48	67	52	100
Netherlands	39	38	61	62	100
Belgium and Luxembourg	60	63	40	37	100

[a] Wood industry and paper pulp and cardboard industries, building materials and glass, metallurgy, metal goods and machinery, electrical machines and appliances, and means of transport.
[b] Agriculture and foodstuffs, chemicals and rubber, clothing, leather and shoes, and textiles.
Source: Compiled by the author.

Finally, the coexistence of autonomous economic policies may have a very important effect.

Consistent Economic Policies

Even between countries that do no belong to a unified area, the measures taken in one country should not be at cross purposes with those taken in the others. Thus, no country should fight against recession by exporting its unemployment if other countries are also experiencing a recession. Yet, a policy that aims at developing exports is good if, in the partner countries, demand exceeds supply.

The search for this consistency in the economic policies of countries with major economic ties is the subject of work being done within the Organization for Economic Cooperation and Development (OECD). But within an economic area that is supposed to be unified, the problem takes on a different dimension, as made clear in the Werner report:

> As a consequence of the progress towards integration the general economic imbalances in the member countries have a direct and immediate effect on the overall develop- ment of the Community. The experience of the last few years has clearly shown that such imbalances may seriously compromise the advance made in the inte- gration of the movements of goods, services and capital. This holds particularly true for the Agricultural Common Market. Taking into account the marked differences which continue to exist between the member countries regarding the accomplishment of the objective of growth and stability, imbalances threaten to arise if we cannot manage to effectively harmonize economic policy.
>
> The increasing interpenetration of economies has led to a weakening in the autonomy of national conjunctural [economic] policies. Mastering economic policy has become all the more difficult since this loss of autonomy at the national level has not been counterbalanced by setting up Community policies. In this the deficiencies and imbalances in the development process of the Common Market show up sharply. [1]

Therefore, manipulating exchange rates cannot be left to the goodwill of each economy without risking the unity of the Common Market. We will thus study how a stability in exchange rates may be ensured, while equilibrating the balance of payments.

For the movements of goods and services, the maintenance of the balance is only possible if the evolution of nominal prices is the same outside and inside the area concerned. This can happen only if the value of the quotient real salary/productivity develops at the same pace in these two economic areas. If this is not the case, there is likely to be a change in the balance of current payments, and restoring the equilibrium can only come about through one of the three following mechanisms: a change in the exchange rate; a drop in the real income in the area with the adverse trade balance; or capital movements. (The writing in this field over the last 20 years has given a more complete description of the mechanisms at work, but here we restrict ourselves to the main points.) Within a single country, the first mechanism does not come into play, since there is a currency unit, and the inevitable equilibria between regions are guaranteed whenever there is an evolution in productivities at different speeds, either through different evolutions of real incomes or through compensating capital movements (for instance, through budgetary flows or social security flows).

Between member countries of an economic union, therefore, there are four possible types of evolution possible (described further on).

It is seen that there can be a stability in exchange rates in one of the following three cases:

1. Rises in productivity, real incomes, and nominal incomes are the same in the different countries.

2. Rises in productivity (and thus in real incomes) are different as are rises in nominal incomes. (The latter is in a proportion that sustains the parallelism of price evolution.)

3. Rises in productivity are equal and those in nominal incomes different, or the reverse, and the equilibrium of the balance of payments is ensured by the capital movements from one country toward another. (As shown in the following table)

Each of these cases will be examined in succession, showing the restrictions they impose on the national governments; this will help to clarify in the section following the unwillingness displayed to take very firm commitments.

In those cases where the rise in productivity is the same in the various countries (the case π Rp and π), it would seem obvious from the start that it should be easy to have a parallelism of the rise in incomes and, thus, of the rise in prices, making the stability in the exchange rates possible.

In practice, things are not so simple, and the maintenance of the parallelism of the rise in nominal incomes (the case π Rp) may run up against serious sociological and political difficulties.

Type of Evolution	Rise in Productivities$^\pi$	Rise in National Incomes	Rise in Prices	Exchange Rates
π Rp	=	=	=	Stable
π π C$_v$ π C$_s$	=	$\neq$	$\neq$	Either variable or stable, with capital movements
R RC$_v$ RC$_s$	$\neq$	=	$\neq$	Either variable or stable, with capital movements
p	$\neq$	$\neq$	=	Stable

= stands for identical evolution in the vaious countries.
$\neq$ stands for different evolutions in the various countries.
Source: Compiled by the author.

First of all, the elasticity of employment in ratio to the rise in prices may be different from one country to the next (technically, the parameters of the Philip's curves are different); in these conditions, the maintenance of the rise in prices below a certain level may give rise to low—and, thus, acceptable—unemployment in one country and much higher unemployment in another. The first country will thus balk at accepting a higher rise in prices, whereas the second will not accept so rigorous a control of prices, which will bring it to an unbearable level of unemployment. Most likely, the origin of these disparities should be sought in the sociological behavior patterns of the various populations (unions and employers).

More generally, inflation is often the least painful political means to ensure ex post macroeconomic equilibrium between those income aspirations—or expenditure aspirations—that are incompatible ex ante with the available production: governments, which are aware of this phenomenon, are basically hesitant to restrict their leeway to turn to this pain-killing medicine, which makes the most diversified adjustments easier.

Lastly, an effective struggle against inflation presupposes that great use be made of the budgetary instrument. Setting an objective price rise ceiling may then considerably restrict the government's liberty in the volume of its budgeted expenditure and in the distribution of this spending. Also, for all these reasons, identical rises in productivity in two countries are not always accompanied by identical rises in prices. The stability in exchange rates between these countries can only be maintained by capital movements, which may be very sizable. But many governments do not feel entirely comfortable with such movements; because if it is an outflow of capital, an

impoverishment of the country and a cutback in investments are
feared, and if it is an inflow, there is a certain suspicion, when faced
with the risk of foreign investments on home soil, that these investments might reduce the country's eceonomic independence. Thus, the
only way out is a change in the exchange rates.

When productivities rise at different rates from one country to
the other, and thus, also, the evolution of incomes in real terms,
there may or may not be the same evolution in nominal terms. It is
not easy to maintain nominal incomes that are different on both sides
of political borders across which economic exchanges are increasing:
setting up the Common Market, which has facilitated the ability to
make comparisons between countries, has made more people aware
of these disparities at a faster rate then before. This may cause
a country with a low growth rate to align its rise in nominal incomes
with the rises in other countries, which may result in a higher rate
of inflation then in neighboring countries. Thus, the same problems
arise for a stability of the exchange rate as those dealt with above.

Cases with variable exchange rates raise relatively fewer
difficulties of implementation; they can bear different rises in prices
and, therefore, leave room for major disparities in the objectives
and means of internal economic policies, and avoid correction by
capital movements.

Each type of evolution, therefore, has drawbacks peculiar
to it. Now, the respective advantages of each must be examined.

The basic question is: Must we make it a strict rule to strive
for fixed exchange rates? The main criteria should be to attain maximum efficiency throughout the Community. In the abstract, permanen
exchange rates would not be necessary for the decisions made by the
economic agents to lead to the desired efficiency. It would be enough
that the economic agents make consistent forecasts. Thus, some
theoreticians think that the mechanism of fixed exchange rates is not
necessary to ensure economic efficiency, because it would always be
possible to fall back on the safety device of futures markets. This
holds partly true for financial transactions but hardly at all for economic decisions, especially investment decisions, because there is
no forward market for wages, few forward markets for raw materials
and none for goods and services sold.

On the other hand, the rigid exchange system—obviously only
to the extent that the compared evolutions of productivities, wages,
and prices make this system possible—makes the task of the economi
agents easier by freeing them of the need to foresee the differences
in the macroeconomic development between countries and by passing
onto the public authorities the task of carrying out the corresponding
economic policy.

Thus, the choice between systems is not guided by theoretical
considerations but by practical ones. If investment and foreign trade

decisions were made by a few dozen large firms in the Community, the flexible rate system would be feasible. But it certainly provides an obstacle to medium-sized and small firms that wish to expand their geographic horizons and, thus, impedes the formation of a truly unified economic area. (Setting up a single price system for agricultural produce, in which there is a great deal of intra-Community trade, is one answer among many to this kind of concern.)

The preceding line of reasoning strongly suggests that a system of fixed exchange rates is a goal at which to be aimed. Therefore, a policy must be clearly defined that will allow this goal to be attained. In practice, this means that the various member states must agree on the acceptable rate of price rises (more a political than an economic choice) and must be able to select the proper measures (a problem of economic understanding) and put them into effect (a problem of their willingness to do so and their actual political power).

There are a few more points that deserve attention: capital movements; the chronological order and speed of the changes that occur; whether or not a single currency unit exists; the organization of the decision-making process; and, last, relations with the rest of the world.

A political decision of large scope has effects on the capital movements that are accepted between countries. Part of these movements may be due to private agents, but another part must be ensured by the public authorities, either through regular flows—which may be the subject of a degree of medium-term planning through the Community budget (for instance, the Agricultural Fund, the Social Fund, or the Regional Fund) or through flows set in motion by a Community mechanism of monetary cooperation to meet unforeseen contingencies.

For a while, a dispute between experts over the best chronological order for the measures to be taken was very much in fashion, setting the "economists" against the "monetarists." The former argued that it was first necessary to set up the instruments intended to ensure the respect of those economic conditions underlying the maintenance of fixed exchange rates, and the latter asked that, first of all, the decision be made to uphold fixed parities, which meant that the necessary economic policies would have to be put into effect. Actually, this was largely a false dispute (which provided the persons in power with an excuse not to make any decisions). Today, agreement has been reached on the necessity to maintain a certain parallelism in the progression on both levels.

However, between the present-day reality and the final solution to be hoped for, there is a glaring difference. The current situation is one characterized by the juxtaposition of economic policies and national monetary policies (which only leads, at the very most, to confrontations) and, as regards the exchange rate, by the possibility not only of fluctuations within the permitted range set by international agreements but also of changes in parities. The final solution is one where there would be a single economic and monetary policy for the Community (even if the use of the instruments might remain varied within certain limits, from country to country) and where the currencies would be irrevocably welded together. To reach the desired solution, there is much ground to be covered and two possible measures to be taken: either a very gradual advance over a period stretchin from 10 to 15 years or a series of sudden jumps toward the end solution.

If within a real economic and monetary union, it is not possible to have several currencies that may fluctuate, monetary union can be accomplished either by coexisting national currencies being firmly welded together or by having a single currency. As the Werner report pointed out, "from the technical point of view, the choice made betwee these two solutions may seem unimportant, but psychological and political considerations argue in favor of adopting a single currency which would make this undertaking irreversible."[2]

The close coordination of economic policies, whether by working out an economic policy or by adopting budgetary or monetary measure:

> makes it necessary to set up or change a certain
> number of Community organs which should take over
> functions belonging till then to the national authorities.
> Two organs seem absolutely essential if the economic
> and monetary policy within the union is to be mastered:
> a decision-making center for economic policy and a
> Community central banking system

Finally, the working of the monetary union inside the Communit demands that fixed parities also be respected in relations with outside countries. This does not mean that a system of fixed parities between Community currencies and the currencies of outside countries is necessary, but that, if there are floating exchange rates in regard to outside countries, all the Community currencies must float together.

The attitude hitherto adopted will now be examined, and we will study the coordination of economic policies (the work done during the first few years) and the beginnings—which are more recent—of monetary union.

ECONOMIC POLICY SEEN AS A COMMON INTEREST

Beginning Economic Developments of the Common Market

The direction taken by economic developments of the first 15 years of the Common Market can be pinpointed by the traditional indicators: production, employment, and prices.

As for production, at no time did it undergo a decline. At the most, there were periods of slowing down, as well as a few cases where it leveled off. The business cycles of the various member countries tended to draw closer, except in Italy, where economic movements apparently moved away from those of the rest of the Community.

The changes in production structures did not have as unfavorable effects as might have been expected on the level of employment. On the contrary, a marked drop in reported unemployment was recorded for 1958 to 1964. The number of people out of work thereafter ran about half the number that had been reached in 1958. [*]

Thus, it was only after 1967 that there was a net growth in unemployment due, as in Germany, to a sag in the business cycle. At the same time, a large-scale reorganization was taking place in industry, leading to a considerable increase in the number of industrial layoffs as the result of mergers, specialization, and conversion. It seems that, from this time onward, there was a more noteworthy gap between the manpower requirements and the qualifications of the manpower offered, one sign of which was the considerable growth in the demand for foreign manpower and in the number of job offers unfilled.

In fact, the movements of workers between one Community country and another, which were already appreciable before 1958, rose very sharply from 1960 onward, even before all the obstacles to the free movement of labor had been removed. Between 1960 and 1965, the annual average was around 210,000 permanent workers. After this, the movement slackened somewhat, despite the facilities offered. In 1970, the number of workers of Community origin in jobs in Community countries other than their own was about 950,000.

---

[*] This holds true for the Community as a whole, except for France, where the reverse is true: there, unemployment mounted regularly after 1958, but it only went over the Community average in 1971 (as far as the statistics are comparable). But the French case is only an aberration on the surface, since it can be explained by the Algerian war (first by the calling up of troops and, later on, by the influx of Algerian French).

The largest contingent of these workers were Italians, who accounted for 80 percent or 90 percent of manpower migrations inside the Community.

Conversely, the supply of manpower from nonmember countries showed almost a continuous increase. Since 1962, they have exceeded the immigration of workers from Community countries; in 1969, they numbered nearly 700,000 workers, or more than 80 percent of total immigration. Thus, though intra-Community movements of manpower contributed to the Community's economic expansion, they did not make it possible to absorb the pockets of unemployment or to satisfy the whole of the manpower requirements. This indicates that the free circulation of workers, which is the indispensable foundation of economic integration, cannot play its appointed role as a catalyst in solving labor-market problems unless it is integrated into an active employment policy. Jobs in the Community offered to foreign workers prove, in fact, more attractive to workers from nonmember countries than to workers without jobs in the other countries of the Community. This seems to indicate that there is no important general problem of underemployment—except in Italy—but rather a need for adapting personnel to the labor requirements of the market and a need for measures to promote the mobility of the available Community manpower.

The level of prices, indicated by the implicit price of the GNP, rose steadily throughout the Community. (See Table 4.2.) It is often thought that the "normal," or acceptable, rate of increase in the general price level falls around 2 percent to 3 percent per annum; thus, the Third Medium-Term Economic Policy Program says that "It seems reasonable to expect an annual average rate of 2.5-3 % for the period 1971-1975, a little below that forecast for international prices. The choice of this rate expresses the Community's resolve to constitute an area of stability."[3]

During the first few years of the Common Market, prices showed an average rise of barely over 3 percent, but the timing and the extent of this inflationary trend were not the same for every country. However, since 1968-69, price rises have been picking up speed, and the pockets of stability are disappearing. This phenomenon, moreover, is not peculiar to the Community countries.

The evolution in export prices may be compared to that in exchange rates. Reasonably, one might expect that for any two countries, the ratio:

A country's export price
B country's export price

would be about the same as the change in parities, whereas the figures (for France, we have taken January 1, 1959, as our starting point, considering the 1958 exchange rate as unreal) reveal great differences

TABLE 4.2

Change in Parities[a] and Price Evolution—Germany,
France, Italy, The Netherlands, Belgium, and the United Kingdom, 1958–70

Factors	Germany	France	Italy	Netherlands	Belgium	United Kingdom
Change in parities (in percent)	+20	−24[b] (−11)[c]	−1	+8	+3	−14
Price index numbers:						
Consumption	134	165 (155)	150	156	136	152
Implicit GNP	146	170 (160)	157	170	142	153
Wholesale prices (industr.al)	113[d]	148	134	124	—	134
Exports	111	132 (119)	114	111	129	136
Imports	101	127 (118)	104	105	128	134

Note: Figures in parentheses refer to the period 1959–70 and reflect the devaluation of the French franc in 1958.

[a] In relation to the European unit of account.

[b] Including the change of January 1, 1959.

[c] Not including the change of January 1, 1959.

[d] Producers' prices.

Source: Compiled by the author.

Germany has revalued its currency in comparison with France, Italy, and The Netherlands, and it is much more than would seem reasonably justified by the evolution in the export price ratio. Conversely, France would seem to have devalued its currency excessively in comparison with its four partners.

In this light, it is understandable why the EEC Commission said, in November 1968, that a devaluation of the French franc was not necessary. Indeed, it seems that, since 1969, parity changes have been due more to a worldwide monetary disorder than to the implementation of any remedy intended to restore economic parities.

It is clear that the Community's economic problems have undergone a considerable transformation over the years. During the first ten years, interventions were necessary to offset slump conditions or an inflationary trend, which usually appeared in only one or two countries. For the last seven or eight years, however, all the countries have become involved in an inflationary process, which is tending to pick up speed. At no time until 1975 was the Community faced with generalized slack economic conditions, and even less with a recession.

In the preceding section, the theoretical analysis demonstrated that the difficulties which most impede the functioning of the Community appear either when there are worldwide monetary disturbances or when there is a great disparity in the price evolutions of the various partners.

These two sources of disorder, especially the second, started to come into play after 1969 or 1970. This makes it necessary to divide the analysis of the measures taken during the last 15 years into two periods: the first 10 or 11 years, characterized by the gradual setting up of systematic consultations on economic measures to be taken, and the years after, which were overshadowed by attempts to bring about a real economic and monetary union. The first period will be examined below, and the second in the section following.

Coordinating Economic Policies

Over the last 15 years, Community action in this field has included the developing of an appropriate institutional framework, an improvement in the understanding of economic developments, identifying and developing instruments of economic policy, and recommendations for the measures to be taken in the different member countries.

From the standpoint of institutions, the following steps should be noted: the setting up of the Monetary Committee provided for in Article 105 of the Treaty (1958); the Economic Policy Committee (early 1960); the Budgetary Policy Committee (1964); and the Committee of Governors of Central Banks (1964).

Then, the increased pace of inflation and the appearance of the monetary crisis (see below) brought about better-organized and more frequent consultations. For this reason, in February 1971, the Council, in the first session, decided to hold three sessions a year and, particularly at the second session, to draw up the quantitative guidelines for draft national budgets of the following year.

A better understanding of economic developments came about by making available monthly indicators, by regularly carrying out surveys among the entrepreneurs, as well as by drawing up and publishing different documents describing and forecasting in this field, more especially, the quarterly reports of the commission on the "Economic Situation of the Community" and on economic budgets.

Regarding instruments of economic policy, we might point out the drawing up of an inventory of available means, the working out of a model for the analysis of the possible repercussions of the different measures, the institutionalizing of preliminary consultations, and the creation, upon the proposal of the Commission, of systems of short-term and medium-term monetary support (see below).

As for the recommendations on the measures to be taken in the different countries, the events of the years 1963, 1964, and 1968, and the situation since 1969 deserve special attention; the first two as examples of periods where important actions were crowned with a certain success and the second two as examples of periods where repeated efforts by the Commission had no noticeable effect.

During the years 1963-64, several member countries—especially Italy, The Netherlands, and Belgium—underwent an increase in the pace of price rises. In Italy, this movement was accompanied by an extraordinary deterioration in the balance of payments. As early as 1963, the Commission had warned of the danger of coming inflationary developments and had proposed some suitable measures to take in this situation. Since the anti-inflationary efforts undertaken by the various member states up to the beginning of 1964 had not been adequate to eliminate the imbalances, in April 1964, the Council adopted a Commission recommendation to invite the member states to follow a rigorous stabilization policy: for the first time in the Community, a common decision defined the priorities among the different economic policy objectives, as well as setting out the general quantitative standards.

In following this recommendation, the measures taken by the various countries proved effective enough, especially in Italy, so that it was not necessary to carry out the procedure that had been started under the provisions of Article 108 of the Treaty or to turn to the mutual assistance of the other members.

The inflationary trend of 1963-64 dropped off toward 1965, but it picked up speed at an even faster rate in 1968 in France and around 1969 in the rest of the Community.

In 1968, in France, the May-June social crisis set off a sharp increase in prices and—particularly following flights of capital—a serious deterioration in the balance of payments. Therefore, the Commission drafted recommendations and proposed (and the Council approved) to grant France mutual assistance as provided for in the Treaty's Article 108. This directive was given a concrete application, which made it possible to stabilize the situation.

The application took the form of measures launched by the Italian government to boost the economy during the second quarter of 1968, the admission on the German market of various loans payable in marks and issued by French public companies, and the implementation of a policy of relatively low interest rates (at least until December 1968) in all the member countries except France.

In contrast to the earlier successes, up till now, the recommendations drawn up since 1969 to deal with the quickening pace of price increases have had almost no effect, despite the attempts to work out a monetary union (which will be studied in a later section). An account of specific measures that were taken or were planned to deal with employment problems will now be presented.

Specific Measures to Deal with Employment

Both the Treaty of Paris and the Treaty of Rome provided for mechanisms intended to mitigate any adverse effects on employment due to reorganizations that were supposed to result from setting up the Common Market. Thus, under the provisions of the ECSC, reconversion loans were granted that reached 250 million ua between 1958 and 1971 and which contributed to the creation of more than 100,000 jobs. Readaption aids (156 million ua) were also allocated, affecting 440,000 ECSC workers.

The actions provided for by the EEC Treaty are smaller in scope, but they may be enlarged.

The European Investment Bank essentially acts by providing loans and guarantees. These were granted for a total of 2.5 billion ua between 1959 and the end of 1972 for the developing of less developed regions, for modernizing plants, and for developing new activities (Article 130 a and b). Out of this total amount, about 1.5 billion ua were spent in Italy, 0.5 billion ua in France, and 0.2 billion ua in Germany. The European Social Fund was set up to promote employment facilities inside the Community and the mobility of workers, both geographically and between different types of jobs.

Until May 1, 1972, the Fund's action was limited to covering 50 percent of the expenditure incurred by member countries or public bodies in providing productive re-employment for unemployed workers by vocational retraining schemes and resettlement aid. Over the period January 1, 1958, to December 31, 1971, the Fund gave assistance in this field to a total of 210 million ua, in the form of payments made after the expenditure had been incurred, for the benefit of 1.5 million unemployed workers. In this initial phase, the Fund operated as an interstate clearing fund for the benefit of unemployed workers; it acted without any overall plan and without leaving scope for the least initiative by the Community itself.

Since May 1, 1972, the Fund has been basically reformed; indeed, the EEC Treaty made express provision for this reform. It is now an active instrument of employment policy, and it has increased resources, with which it should contribute to making the best use of the whole active population under a scheme of priorities laid down at Community level. Hereafter, two kinds of interventions are provided for: the first are primarily complementary to Council decisions, whenever Community policies affect or may affect the employment level. The second are not related to Council decisions and aim at mitigating those situations most worrying from the employment standpoint, particularly in regions lagging behind in development or declining, and in some branches of economic activity especially concerned with technical progress or with important changes in production conditions or the placing of goods. Those initiatives that may profit from the Fund's assistance may henceforth originate either in the public sector or its equivalent or in the private sector. Furthermore, the appropriations of the Fund are rapidly growing (They amounted to 223 million ua in 1973.)

BEGINNINGS OF MONETARY UNION

The Community's monetary problems were discussed comparatively little by the public authorities during the first years of the Common Market because they hardly seemed to be the most important problems: moreover, in this field, the Treaty laid down neither any specific courses of action nor any precise deadlines. The chapter on monetary policy included in the Commission's memorandum (October 1962) on the Community's program of action during the second stage remained the only one of its kind. As late as the time of the merging of the Community "executives" (July 1967), very little was being undertaken, except for studies and discussions.

It was the monetary events of 1968 and 1969 (see Table 4.3) that forced those in power to seriously consider taking action, by demonstrating that it was impossible to continue on the basis of such a loose coordination of economic decisions taken at the national

TABLE 4.3

Crises and Decisions in Monetary Matters, 1968-74

Date	Crisis	Proposal	Decision taken
November 1968	Alarm over the franc		
February 1969		Commission memorandum	
August 1969	Devaluation of the French franc		
October 1969	Revaluation of the German mark		
December 1969			The Hague Summit Conference; principle established of an Economic and Monetary Union to be set up by Stages
February 1970			Central banks; agreement on the system of short-term monetary support
October 1970		The Werner report	
February 1971			Council decision; Agreement on setting up the Economic and Monetary Union by stages; intensification of periodic consultations; fluctuations limited (the "snake"; the principle of medium-term financial assistance
May 1971	The German mark crisis—floating of the mark and the florin		
August 1971	Nixon decisions Different reactions in the Community		
December 1971			Washington agreement
January 1972		Commission communication to the Council	
March 1972			Council; narrowing of the margins; use of Community currencies; regulation of international financial flows
June 1972	The Pound crisis— floating of the pound		
September 1972			Finance ministers; principle of a European Monetary Cooperation Fund established
October 1972			Paris Summit Conference; Reaffirmation of the economic and monetary union; timetable drawn up
February 1973	Devaluation of the dollar		
March 1973	German mark crisis		Council; Community currencies to float together vis-a-vis the dollar; strengthening of control over disturbing capital movements; the European Monetary Cooperation Fund set up
April 1973			
January 1974	Floating of the French franc		

Source: Compiled by the author.

level. As a matter of fact, the monetary decisions made by Germany
and France in November 1968, and then in the second quarter of
1969, and the French devaluation in August followed by the German
devaluation in October were taken without any organized consultation
with their Common Market partners. For this reason, on February
12, 1969, the Commission sent the Council a ground-laying memorandum (sometimes called "the Barre Plan") on the coordination of
economic policies and monetary cooperation within the Community.
This memorandum has three basic theses:

1. The first need is for national medium-term orientations to
follow the same line. The main medium-term objectives to be defined
by common agreement among the member countries relate to the
rate of growth in production and employment, the evolution of prices,
and the balance of (current) payments. These fundamental objectives
are closely linked and must be determined at the same time.
2. Within the framework of these guidelines, concerted short-
term economic policies must be implemented. Therefore, it seems
necessary to place the stress on coordinating economic and current
financial policies in order to be able to foresee economic disequilibria,
and should these arise, to combat them in the most effective manner.
Prevention plays a more important role in a multinational area that
is in the process of becoming integrated and whose tariff policy vis-
a-vis outside countries is comparatively moderate than it does in a
national economy that is relatively closed to the outside. Indeed,
it is to the common interest to avoid or mitigate as quickly as possible any disequilibrium, even if it occurs within a single country,
since the risk of contagion to the whole Community is great.
3. Even given the preceding concerted efforts, "accidents along
the way" are not in the least out of the question. This means that a
mechanism of monetary cooperation must be set up that will act within the framework of jointly defined objectives of medium- and short-
term economic policy, mechanisms intended to avoid the worsening
of disequilibria rather than to mitigate the effects of crises that have
already broken out. A member state in difficulty should be able to
get from its Community partners, at the right moment and without
delay, the financing to help it meet its difficulties, without jeopardizing
the functioning of the Common Market. This financing alone will not
suffice to correct the observed disequilibria, but it will enable the
receiving country to put the necessary measures into effect in the
best possible conditions.

These three themes are found in all the later documents, resolutions, and decisions.
As regards the coordination of medium-term economic policies,
the third program—as shown—stressed harmonization of those

objectives that particularly had to do with full employment and price stability: this third program which was more than a medium-term development program, stressed the maintenance of medium-term equilibrium.

As regards the coordination of short-term policies, the February 1969 document emphasized the necessity of making the already existing consultations more systematic, so as to go beyond, in the question of draft budgets, the simple exchange of views within the Budgetary Policy Committee. What was hoped was to develop a meaningful encounter between ministers, an encounter that would deal only with the great masses of expenditure and receipts and with their impact on economic growth and equilibrium, judged particularly in the light of those objectives pursued on a medium-term basis.

Lastly, as regards the Community mechanism of monetary cooperation, the Commission distinguished between short-term monetary support and medium-term financial assistance. On the first point, it had this to say:

> Every participating country commits itself to making available to the others resources not to exceed a certain limit. The indebtedness of each participant with respect to the others which results from implementing the system may exceed a certain limit.
>
> Any recourse to this system by a participating country should be followed up as soon as possible by a consultation with the appropriate Community authorities. The purpose of this consultation will be to determine in the light of the receiving country's situation what actions are called for, both for this country and the other member countries.

It will be noted that the guarantees proposed for this short-term monetary support cannot be extended indefinitely unless the country concerned takes the necessary steps to re-establish the equilibrium.

After the discussions throughout 1969, an important political impetus came out of the Hague Summit Conference. In the conference's final communique, this passage stood out:

> They [the heads of state or of the government] . . . have agreed that within the Council . . . a plan will be worked out during 1970 with a view to setting up an economic and monetary union.
>
> The development of monetary cooperation should be founded on the harmonization of economic policies.

> They have agreed to examine the possibility of instituting
> a European Reserve Fund which should result from a
> economic and monetary policy.

The term economic and monetary union, which came into such common
use, became in this way official.

On February 9, 1970, the agreement on the short-term monetary support went into force. The total assistance provided for
amounted to 1 billion ua, with the chance of a maximum of an additional billion.

Then, on March 6, 1970, applying Point 8 of the Hague Resolution, the Council decided that a committee, presided over by Minister
Werner from Luxembourg, should be put in charge of working out
a report that would include an analysis of the different suggestions
and would make it possible to select those options for setting up the
Community's economic and monetary union. The Werner report consisted of three main points: an account of the reasons why new efforts
were needed (reasons already discussed above); an account of the
"final state" to be attained; and the position of the principle of putting
the plan into effect through stages, and a statement of the actions
needed in the first stage.

In its final state, the Economic and Monetary Union would make
possible an area inside which goods and services, as well as persons
and capital, would move freely, without distortions in competition
and without giving rise to structural or regional disequilibria.

A monetary union implies the total and irreversible converta-
bility of currencies, the elimination of the margins of fluctuations
in exchange rates, the fixing of absolutely permanent parity ratios,
and the complete freeing of capital movements. Such a union could
either keep the national monetary signs in use or create a new single
Community currency. From the technical point of view, it may seem
unimportant which avenue is followed, but political and psychological
considerations argue in favor of adopting a single currency, which
would emphasize the irreversibility of the action.

The need to fix permanent parity ratios made itself felt in 1969,
when the French devaluation and the German revaluation started to
have repercussions on the common agricultural market. To avoid
abrupt changes in farmers' incomes, in the way of a drop in France
and an increase in Germany, and yet to maintain the principle of
price unity throughout Community territory, a temporary adjustment
process had to be set up. This was done by temporarily putting into
effect export (or import) taxes on goods to other member countries
and subsidies to imports (or exports) coming from other member
countries. If the problem was less glaring for industrial goods, it
was because a single price system was not imposed on the whole of

the Community economy. However, if a better use of the factors of production is hoped for, such a price system must gradually be set up. Furthermore, the economic agents will only be fully convinced that the whole Community constitutes a single market when they are guaranteed that there will be absolutely no changes in parity ratios within the economic union.

In such a union, only the overall Community balance of payments in relation to the outside world is important. At this stage, the Community's internal equilibrium will have been accomplished, just as inside a national territorial unit, thanks to the free movement of the factors of production and to financial transfers from the public and private sectors.

Within such an economic union, by definition, there is no longer a balance-of-payments problem. However, those price disparities that may arise between one part of the territory and another give rise to movements of production factors, particularly capital, which make possible medium-term adjustments through regional relocation of production. In the short-term, these disparities may entail some firms closing down and some unemployment. Thus, it is very important that an identical evolution of prices be maintained throughout the Community territory. To the extent that public budgetary or monetary measures can influence the general price level, it is important that these public measures within one country be perfectly consistent one with the other. This means that a certain number of conditions must be respected in a unified economic and monetary union.

The main conditions are that:

1. liquidity creation within the area as a whole, as well as monetary policy and credit, all be centralized.

2. monetary policy in regard to the outside world be under Community jurisdiction.

3. the member states' policies in regard to capital markets be unified.

4. the essential figures of all public budgets, and in particular any variation in their volume, the extent of the balances, and the means of financing or the ways these means may be used are to be decided at the Community level.

5. the structural and regional policies no longer be exclusively the jurisdiction of the member countries.

6. a systematic and continual consultation of the social partners be ensured at the Community level.

All this would necessitate major institutional reforms: setting up a single decision-making center for economic policy and instituting a Community system of central banks.

Because it was aware that these objectives could not be attained in a short period of time, the Werner report put forward the principle of accomplishing these goals step by step, while stressing that the measures that were necessary were interdependent and that there should be a certain parallelism between the development of monetary unification and that of the unification of economic policies. It stressed as well that, at the same time as the member states' autonomy in economic policy was being reduced, the corresponding powers would have to be developed at the Community level.

There are two remarks to be made about this report. First of all, it is extremely consistent. Even if the details may be debated, the line of reasoning is faultless. This is why some of the criticisms directed against it have questioned the very starting point, that is, the necessity for fixed and immutable exchange rates among the currencies of the various countries, or, what amounts to the same thing, the adoption of a single currency. This questioning comes mainly from persons who are convinced that it is enough to have a free trade area completed by some coordination of economic policies.

The second remark concerns the surprisingly reticent way in which the report deals with international monetary problems. It is true that the intensification of cooperation over external monetary policy is discussed, and it is said that a first step must be made toward gradually setting up an EEC representative unit to the International Monetary Fund (IMF) and the other financial authoritative bodies. It is equally true that it speaks of an experimental de facto limitation of the fluctuations of exchange rates between Community currencies, to be implemented at the beginning of the first stage and to operate within margins narrower than those resulting from the application of the margins that were in force vis-a-vis the dollar at the time the system was introduced. This objective is to be reached by concerted action on the dollar. But no hint is given as to what form this concerted action might take. In this, the report is too reticent, even if such reticence is understandable politically (which explains why the decisions made in February 1971 were not going to hold up in the face of the events of May 1971).

On the basis of this report, presented October 8, 1970, the Council made a very important decision on February 8-9, 1971. In particular, it said that

the Council and the Representatives of the Governments of the Member States express their political will to introduce, in the course of the next ten years, an economic and monetary union, in accordance with a phased plan commencing on 1 January 1971.

The measures to be carried out must be such that at the end of this process the Community shall:

1. Constitute a zone within which persons, goods, services, and capital will move freely and without distortion of competition, without, however, giving rise to structural or regional imbalances, and in conditions which will allow persons exercising economic activity to operate on a Community scale;

2. form an individual monetary unit within the international system characterised by the total and irreversible convertibility of currencies, the elimination of fluctuation margins of rates of exchange and the irrevocable fixing of parity rates—all of which are indispensable conditions for the creation of a single currency—and including a Community organisation of the Central Banks;

3. hold the powers and responsibilities in the economic and monetary field enabling its Institutions to organize the administration of the union. To this end, the required economic policy decisions shall be taken at Community level and the necessary powers shall be given to the Institutions of the Community.

Powers and responsibilities shall be distributed between the Institutions of the Communities, on the one hand, and the Member States, on the other hand, in accordance with the requirements for the cohesion of the union and the efficiency of Community action.

The final state defined is thus quite clear: currencies irrevocably welded together and Community economic policy. In some ways this text acts to complete the Treaty of Rome.

It is also made clear that the advance toward this state is to be made through stages. Thus, those who supported a great jump forward found their approach rejected.

Furthermore, a calender of no longer than three years was planned for the first phase. Within those three years, two major measures were called for: (1) intensifying and generalizing compulsory prior consultations and a reinforcement of the coordination of short-term economic policies; and (2) from the beginning of the phase and by way of experiment, to keep fluctuations in the rates between Community currencies within margins narrower than those resulting from the application of the margins in force for the U.S. dollar, by means of concerted action vis-a-vis this currency.

This last point came to be called "keeping the snake in the tunnel".* In the face of the various concerns mentioned in the precedi

---

* In the international monetary system as it was set up by the Bretton Woods agreements in 1944, the exchange rates were fixed but

theoretical section, this course of action was intended to deal with problems connected with external exchange markets. As a matter of fact, this shrinking of the margins acts in the short term, but it does not change the possibility that, over slightly longer periods, there may be fluctuations of the rates.

On the same day, the Council agreed to the introduction of a medium-term financial assistance mechanism that completed the agreement of February 9, 1970, on the system of short-term monetary support. The sums made available were increased to $2 billion. "Now the Community has at its disposal a flexible and effective mechanism which represents the first example of monetary solidarity organized within the Community."[4]

Finally, the Council decided as well on measures intended to lead to closer coordination of short-term policies and stronger collaboration between the central banks.

Such a series of decisions provided answers to the questions raised by the Commission in its memorandum of February 1969. Indeed, the sums allocated for the short-term support were modest, and the coordination procedures still had too little force; yet, these seemed to be sound beginnings.

As of May 1971, these fine resolutions have been sorely put to the test. Faced by waves of capital inflows during the first days of May, the exchanges were closed in Germany, The Netherlands, and Belgium, as well as in Switzerland. The Community consultation procedures went into action. In particular, the Commission took a stand against a revaluation of all Community currencies, which was considered ill-timed. It also opposed a free fluctuation of Community currencies in relation to the dollar or having recourse to a moderate widening of the fluctuation margins of the Community currencies, both of which were considered as likely to create speculation. The

---

a slight margin of fluctuation was permitted. Furthermore, each currency's exchange rate was defined in relation to the dollar. The result was that the margins of fluctuation between any two European currencies (for example, the French franc and the Deutschmark) were twice as big as those for each currency in relation to the dollar.

The objective of the mechanism that was baptized the "Snake" was to hold down the margins of fluctuation (theoretically, to reduce them by half). This implied concerted actions by the monetary authorities of the countries concerned. Thus it is said that a currency belongs to the "Snake" if its fluctuations in relation to the dollar (around a fixed parity) are maintained within limits consistent with the fluctuations of the "Snake's" other currencies.

Commission proposed rather that the member states officially affirm
their absolute determination not to change their parities and that they
take a series of measures to support this determination.

In fact, it turned out to be impossible to come to an agreement
on a common course of action. As of May 10, the German mark was
floated, whereas Belgium put the two-tier exchange system into
operation, and nothing was changed for the French franc and the
lira, all of this with the kind blessings of the Council.

As Barre was to explain a short time later:

> First of all it must be acknowledged that the Community's
> consultation procedures have been complied with. The
> consultations, however, did not result in the choice of
> Community measures but made it possible to take note,
> in a Community framework, of the unilateral measures
> and to limit their impact on the Community.
>
> This situation was not the result of ill-will on the
> part of one or the other country, nor were there ulterior
> motives. It derives from the dissimilarity of the situations,
> and consequently of the interests, of the various countries
> within the Community, from disagreement among member
> countries on economic doctrine, and from differing
> viewpoints on the methods to be used to solve inter-
> national monetary problems. [5]

But this May alarm was only a beginning. On August 15, 1971,
President Nixon announced some dramatic measures, particularly
suspending the convertibility of the dollar (which, in any case, was
already inconvertible in fact), the levying of a 10 percent surtax on
imports, and tax relief for home investments and exports. Faced with
these decisions, the consultations between member countries intensified greatly (as well as those with the future EEC members). If, on
one hand, it was not at all difficult to agree to censure the American
aimed at keeping the quotations for commercial operations and those
reform of the international monetary system, on the other hand, it
proved impossible to take a common stand on Community currencies.
However, the Monetary Committee had said that two broad solutions
were possible for the EEC countries: either a free but joint floating
of the six currencies as a group, keeping the current fluctuations
margins, or narrowing them if necessary, or, on the contrary, to
set up a two-tier system of exchange everywhere, which would be
aimed at keeping the quotations for commercial operations and those
for financial transactions as separate as possible.

Both solutions were adopted at the same time, but one by some
countries and the other by other countries: (1) the German mark and

the florin continued to float (as well as the pound, the Swiss franc, and the yen); (2) the two-tier system was applied in France and Belgium (with the floating of the Belgian commercial franc); and (3) in Italy, the lira floated within rather narrow limits.

On December 18, 1971, the Washington agreement brought back a minimum of order to the situation by setting new relations in exchange rates in the form of parities or central rates and a temporary widening of the margins of fluctuation of the exchange rates to 2.25 percent above or below the new exchange rates. Lastly, the new realignment of currencies was completed by abolishing the surtax and the discriminatory measures that had been set up or planned by the U.S. government on August 15, 1971.

This improvement in the situation, however, was far from solving all the problems for the Community, a fact stressed in the Commission communication to the Council on January 12, 1972: it stated that authorizing the widening of the margins of fluctuation on the international level could seriously disturb intra-Community trade, since no measure had been taken to ensure the eventual reconvertibility of the dollar and no arrangements had been made to move toward regulation of the international capital market.

Thus, on the basis of Commission proposals, new decisions were made. On March 21, the Council invited "the Central Banks of the Member States to reduce, progressively, while making full use of the fluctuation margins allowed by the IMF on a world plane, the gap existing at any given moment between the exchange rates of the strongest and the weakest currencies of the Member States."[*]

---

[*] The text continues to say:

> To this end, for a first period during which these procedures will be tested, the Central Banks are asked to intervene on their respective foreign exchange markets in accordance with the following principles:
>
> a) As from a date to be fixed by the Governors of the Central Banks, interventions shall be effected in Community currencies, on the basis of the margins recorded on the markets at that date;
>
> b) As these limits converge, the margins mentioned under a) above shall be narrowed down and shall no longer be widened;
>
> c) By 1st July 1972 at the latest, the gap existing at any given time between the currencies of two Member States may not exceed 2.25%.

Three steps had thus been taken: one avoided a step backward by tightening once again the fluctuation margins of the Community currencies; another was a new action and established the principle of using Community currencies in the dollar's stead; and the third initiated a control over movements of floating capital between the Community and the nonmember countries. It was thought in this was that the Community was moving toward a situation where it could constitute an area of free convertibility and monetary stability within the international monetary system.

This hope was short-lived. On June 23, because of the massive speculative pressure brought to bear on the pound sterling, the British government decided to let its currency temporarily float. Great Britain did not feel itself capable of respecting either the commitments made in the Washington agreements or the Community monetary arrangements. The damage was of limited extent in that the Six held fast to their commitments, with the exception of Italy, which received authorization to intervene for a limited time in dollars instead of Community currency in order to keep the lira within the Community "Snake."

The next step was taken in September 1972, when the finance ministers agreed to set up a European Monetary Cooperation Fund (EMCF), an agreement that was confirmed at the Paris Summit Conference in October 1972.

---

2) To this end, the Central Banks are asked to intervene in the foreign currency markets of their own countries, in accordance with the following principles:

—in Community currencies, if their levels reach, on the foreign currency market involved, the maximum limit of fluctuation authorized under Point 1:

—in U.S. dollars, if the rate of exchange of the dollar reaches, on the foreign exchange market involved, the maximum fluctuation limit authorized under IMF rules;

—within these fluctuation limits, only after a concerted decis on of the Central Banks. . . .

5) With a view to discouraging excessive capital inflows and to neutralizing their adverse effects on internal liquidity, the Council approves the directive for the regulation of international cash flows and the neutralisation of their undesirable effects on internal liquidity, proposed by the Commission on 23 June 1971.

The declaration adopted at this meeting served to officially reaffirm various points agreed upon at the previous meetings of the Council or of the finance ministers.[*]

The timetable was thus set up for the various tasks to be accomplished.

As early as January 1973, the Commission sent the Council a proposal asking that the European Monetary Cooperation Fund be set up.

But in early February, a new monetary crisis arose with an influx of dollars into Germany. This crisis was to result in the devaluation of the dollar by 10 percent on February 12 and in the decision by Italy (which had instituted a two-tier exchange system

---

[*] The text reads:

1) The Heads of State and Government reaffirm the resolve of the Member States of the enlarged Community to move irrevocably toward the Economic and Monetary Union, by confirming all the details of the Acts passed by the Council and by the Member States representatives on 22 March 1971 and 21 March 1972.

The required decisions will have to be taken during 1973 to allow transition to the second stage of the Economic and Monetary Union on 1 January 1974 and in view of its complete realization by 31 December 1980 at the latest.

The Heads of State and Government reaffirmed the principle of parallel progress in the various fields of the Economic and Monetary Union.

2) They declared that fixed but adjustable parities between their currencies are an essential basis for achieving the Union and expressed their resolve to set up mutual defence and support mechanisms within the Community, which will allow the Member States to ensure that they are honoured.

They decided to set up officially a European Monetary Cooperation Fund before 1 April 1973. Based on the EEC Treaty, the Fund will be run by the Governors Committee of the Central Banks within the overall guidelines of economic policy adopted by the Council of Ministers. In its early stage the Fund will function on the following basis:

a) Concertation between the Central Banks over the required shrinkage of fluctuation margins between

in January) and Japan to let their currencies float. Drawing its
lessons from this new crisis, the Commission once again strongly
stressed the necessity of an effective control on short-term capital
movements across the Community's borders.

The highly relevant nature of such a stand was confirmed in
early March, since a new wave of speculation was launched against
the dollar, resulting in the closing of the exchange markets from
March 2 to March 19. This time, the governments took more dras-
tic measures, since on March 12, the Council took the following
decisions:

1) to keep the maximum spot variance between the
D.M., the Danish crown, the florin, the Belgian franc,
the Luxembourg franc and the French franc at 2.25 %. For
Member States keeping a two-tier system of exchange
this commitment applies only to the regulated market;
2) to release the Central Banks from having to
intervene in the fluctuation margins of the U.S. dollar;
3) to apply more strictly the Directive of 21 March
1972 and set up whatever additional monitoring devices
may be necessary so as to shelter the system from
disruptive capital movements.

––––––––––––

their currencies.
b) Multilateralizing of positions arising from
intervention in Community currencies and multilateralizing inter-Community rules.
c) Utilization for the above of a European monetary unit of account.
d) Administration of short-term monetary
support between the Central Banks.
e) The very short-term financing of the Agreement
on shrinking the margins and short-term monetary
support will be regrouped within the Fund through an
updated mechanism. For this, the short-term monetary support will be adjusted technically without changing
its basic character or the consultation procedures involved.
The competent Community agencies will have to
submit reports.
a) On short-term aid dealings by 30 September latest;
b) On terms for progressive pooling of reserves by
31 December 1973.

The British, Irish and Italian members said that
their Governments intended to back as soon as possible
the decision to keep the Community fluctuation margins.

Yet, once again, the measures taken were insufficient, and the
Community structure remained fragile. All that was needed was an
external event, such as the quadrupling of the price of crude oil, to
convulse the Community and prevent it from advancing to the second
significant stage of the Economic and Monetary Union.

In fact, the March 1971 resolution hoped that the second stage
of the Economic and Monetary Union would be started on January 1,
1974, with the adoption of far more restrictive measures. The delay
in putting into effect the measures planned for the first stage inter-
rupted this progression. In December 1973, the Commission proposed
a series of decisions that were relatively modest in scope and which
the Council was to adopt in February 1974:

1. the decision regarding the achievement of a higher degree of con-
vergence of the economic policies of the member states of the EEC;
2. the directive concerning stability, growth, and full employment
within the Community;
3. the decision setting up an Economic Policy Committee; and
4. the resolution concerning a short-term monetary support.

Except for the last two points, these decisions were drafted in
very general terms, which left each country the freedom to interpret
them broadly and rather differently, thus restricting the governments'
actions very little.

In January 1974, France, subjected to strong speculation against
the franc and refusing the financial assistance offered by Germany,
decided to let the franc float temporarily (which led it to cancel the
two-tier exchange system in March 1974). When re-examining the
problem six months later, as planned, France came to the conclusion
that the necessary conditions did not exist to enable it to rejoin the
"Snake"; this only happened officially in July 1975, to be followed by
its leaving the "Snake" again in March 1976.

In May 1974, faced with the deterioration of its balance of payments, the Italian government adopted safeguard measures on the
basis of Article 109 of the Rome Treaty (setting up a compulsory cash
deposit, interest free, corresponding to 50 percent of the value of
imports, for products representing about 40 percent of total Italian
purchases from abroad). Since the Council refused to grant the normal Community assistance, the Commission authorized the Italian
measures. On the other hand, the short-term monetary support of
1.5 billion ua that was granted in March 1973 was rolled over to

September, and then again to December 1974. Then, in November 1974, a medium-term financial assistance was granted, amounting to 1.1 billion ua for three and a half years.

Concerning the functioning of Community mechanisms, attention should be drawn to the firm warning of the Commission on June 6, 1974. A similar alarm sounded in the president's communication before the Council on September 16:

> In face of the situation, Europe must react. The future of the Community and the interests of each of its members are at stake. This is no longer the time to seek out pretexts or explanations for a lack of action in the very real difficulties of the present situation. We must begin to act without any further delay. We must simultaneously strengthen and adapt the intra-Community financial mechanisms and give Europe its proper role in re-establishing the world economic order and that of the international monetary system.

Then, the president suggested measures to be taken, in the form of Community loans, a new monetary unit of account, Community joint-float arrangements, an adaptation of the intra-Community exchange apparatus, and coordinated action on the functioning of the Euromarkets.

The principle of issuing a Community loan whose proceeds would then be lent out to those member states facing a disequilibrium in their balance of payments due to the hike in the prices of oil products was decided in October 1974, and the negotiations over the issuing of a first loan were started in 1975. Even if the maximum ($3 billion) is modest, it stands as an important decision because it gives concrete form to the resolve to put the Community's might, through Community action, at the service of those member states that are most in need of its aid.

The European unit of account (EUA) is defined by all the fixed amounts of the nine currencies following (based on 1976 exchange rates):

Currencies	Percentage in EUA	Percent
Deutsche mark	0.828	27.3
Pound (United Kingdom)	0.0885	17.5
Franc (France)	1.15	19.5
Lit.	109.0	14.0
Florin	0.286	9.0
FB	3.66	7.9
Flux.	0.14	0.3
DKr.	0.217	3.0
Pound (Ireland)	0.00759	1.5

In the present monetary situation, the main advantage offered
by the Eua is threefold: to have a value calculated each day on the
basis of the exchange rates of the currencies involved; to reflect the
Community monetary identity; and to serve as a milestone on the way
to the Monetary Union.

The major proposals made by the Commission in December 1974
to strengthen the EMCF were adopted in 1976. On the other hand,
no measures were undertaken regarding the Europmarkets.

On the whole, the situation during 1976 may be summarized as
follows:

1. There was agreement on the principle of fixed but adjustable
parities. However, floating of currencies did occur—the pound
sterling, the Irish pound, the Italian lira, and the French franc.

2. There was agreement on a shrinking of the fluctuation margins (the "Snake"), but this currently only exists between currencies
more or less closely linked to the deutsche mark.

3. There was agreement on preferential use of Community
currencies for the functioning of the "Snake", as well as a waiver for
the lira.

4. There was agreement for a short-term monetary support
mechanism, but the allocation was far too inadequate to meet serious
crises.

5. There was agreement on a joint European floating vis-a-vis
the dollar.

6. There was agreement on a European Monetary Cooperation
Fund, but it was to play only a modest role in European monetary
affairs.

7. There was agreement on the principle of a control over flows
of floating capital (very inadequately enforced, in fact).

Thus, over the desired goals, agreement has been reached on
the most important points. There has been very real improvement
when one considers that the different points of view have been drawing
closer together.

However, the experience of the last few years shows that the
best of intentions, even when stated in official terms, have difficulty
bearing up under pressure when there is a lack of adequate instruments
and sufficient willpower. Of what importance are the $2 billion of
the short-term support mechanism in face of a Eurodollar market of
several tens of billions of dollars (as of the end of 1976, around
$180 billion), a market that is still under the control of the public
authorities to a very slight degree. * As for the coordinated economic

---

* Thus, the Bundesbank had to take up $2.2 billion in one
week in early May 1971, $5.9 billion between January 1 and

policies that would be necessary, as we have seen above, in order
to make a monetary union possible, it would take an agreement on
the priorities among the magic triangle's objectives: full employment,
price stability, and equilibrium of balance of payments. This is still
far off and is hindered as well by the various difficulties listed in the
preceding section.

Finally, this brief historical survey shows that the governments
decide only very slowly to take the necessary measures; experience
must prove over and over again that the decisions adopted are insufficient before a real step ahead will be made. Only when the floating
of the German mark failed to stop speculation was the principle of
fixed but adjustable parities accepted; it was then completed by various
measures of mutual assistance. Then, only when this also proved
insufficient and it was recognized that the crises were not the result
of a structural imbalance in exchange rates but were specifically
speculative in nature were measures taken. While awaiting the reform
of the international monetary system, two measures have been adopted
that may maintain a minimum of stability in the Community, namely,
a joint floating of currencies vis-a-vis the outside world and the
beginning of control over movements of floating capital. How many
more crises will it take before this control is made really effective?

In terms of economic cycles, European construction has been
singularly favored by chance. In fact, of the two disasters that might
have threatened it, economic recession and inflation, the first has
never appeared, except in 1975, and the second only came on the
scene after about 12 years, affecting the rest of the world at the same
time.

No one will ever know how the Community would have stood
up to a general economic decline that would have hit all the European
countries simultaneously. Would it have been caught up in a general
retreat by each country into its own problems, trying to export its
unemployment or at least trying to keep from importing that of its
neighbor? Or on the contrary, in face of this challenge, would it have
been caught up in the impetus of a joint search for an effective defense
The progress made in both economic understanding and political resolve has made it possible for the governments to put into effect the
measures necessary for maintaining expansion and have thus protected
the Community from possible fatal blows. Inflation, however, is a
greater danger in that its effects are only felt slowly: five years in
this regard is a fairly short period.

Thus, the fact that the Community institutions have taken up
the problem of macroeconomic policies some time after the setting

---

January 9, 1973, and $2.8 billion on March 1, 1973.

up of a large market—following in this regard the priorities laid down
in the Treaty—has not had serious repercussions.

But as regards the decision-making process in the Community,
the developments of the last few years have been equally instructive.
The current mechanism is only very inadequately adapted to rapid
decision making in a field where emergencies are frequent, as well
as to bold decision making in a field where circumstances change at
dazzling speed.

The report of the study group "Economic and Monetary Union
1980," presided over by R. Marjolin (presented in March 1975)
stressed all these inadequacies and laid the blame for the failure of
the European Monetary Union on three main factors:

1. unfavorable events: the international monetary crisis, the
financial crisis which followed the increase in oil prices, but above
all;

2. the lack of any European resolve: in face of the crisis, the
governments acted in a national way and "attemps to cope with the
different crises by joint action have been hesitant and have not been
followed up."[6]

3. "inadequate understanding of what an E.M.U. is, and the
conditions which must be fulfilled before it can see the light of day
and start functioning."[7]

The main condition to be fulfilled in order to bring about the
European Monetary Union is therefore that "the national governments
turn over to joint institutions all the instruments of monetary policy
and economic policy which should be utilized throughout the Community." The institutions should as well "have discretionary powers
similar to those the national governments currently enjoy in order
to be able to cope with unforeseen events."[8] In underlining the necessity for a Community decision-making center, the report fell in with
some of the conclusions of the Werner plan. On the other hand, the
group questioned the "idea that a European economic and monetary
policy could come into being almost imperceptibly" and wondered
whether the condition necessary for the European Monetary Union
would not rather be "a total and almost instantaneous change."[9]

Finally, the group concluded that a joint resolve was needed in
the face of the current problems of inflation, unemployment, and the
balance of payments, and that this joint resolve was mandatory if discussions on the European Monetary Union were to be continued.

In conclusion, it might be added that some of this hesitation
to go ahead stems from the fact that monetary policy not only involves
aspects internal to the Community but also aspects external to it, on
which the various countries' attitudes are still far from being similar,
as will be seen in the next chapter.

NOTES

1. Rapport au Conseil et à la Commission concernant la réalization par étapes de l'Union economique et monétaire dans la Communaute (Rapport Werner) (1970).

2. Ibid.

3. Official Journal 50, no. 49 (March 1, 1971): 20.

4. R. Barre, editorial, Bulletin of the European Communities, no. 3 (1970).

5. R. Barre (Report given before the European Parliament, May 18, 1971).

6. R. Marjolin, "Economic and Monetary Union 1980" (March 1975).

7. Ibid.

8. Ibid.

9. Ibid.

5

THE COMMUNITY AND THE
REST OF THE WORLD

At the outset, it must be stated that the Treaty objectives are
presented here in very general terms. The field covered is one that
is closely linked with foreign policy; it is therefore prudent to avoid
entanglement in unduly precise statements. The relevant texts are
chiefly concerned with the progressive elimination of restrictions
on international trade and with solidarity between the Community and
the Overseas Countries and Territories. The main instruments
specifically mentioned are the setting up of a common customs tariff,
a common commercial policy in dealing with nonmember countries,
procedures to mitigate disequilibria in the balance of payments, and
association with the Overseas Countries and Territories with a view
to increasing trade and pursuing a joint campaign of economic and
social development.

In practice, the Community has been confronted during its
existence, in common with other countries, with four great international economic problems. These are the liberalization of world trade,
the contribution to the development of the developing countries, the
re-establishment of a world monetary order, and the choice of the
attitude to be taken with respect to foreign investments and the part
to be played by multinational companies.

The first three of these problems have been raised and debated
in international organizations; the fourth has only been touched upon.
Only the first, however, has received a fairly substantial answer.
Since all four of these problems are extremely important, it would
be as well to identify the reasons for the absence of response to three
of them and to see how far the Community has suffered from this.

The following examination will, therefore, be centred on these
essential questions:

1. How were the common customs tariff and the common commercial policy brought into existence; what were the effects on the Community's external trade; and how was the balance of payments achieved between the Community and the rest of the world?

2. What action has the Community taken to help the developing countries?

3. What contribution has the Community made to the organization and the administration of international economic relations?

POLICY OF OPENING UP TOWARD THE WORLD

Currently, the Community's commercial and economic relations with the rest of the world are organized as follows:

1. With the industrialized countries having a market economy (the United States, Canada, Japan, and other European and Western countries), commercial relations are carried out traditionally within the framework of the General Agreement on Tariffs and Trade (GATT) regulations and with a moderate common external tariff (see below).

2. With countries with a state-run trade, these consist mainly of commercial exchanges, but also, and increasingly, of transfers of technology. These exchanges are made in the framework of agreements and annual plans concluded at the level of the public authorities. The Treaty's principle on this is that the Community's commercial policy is a common policy; agreements should therefore be negotiated and signed by the Community constituting a single legal entity. The USSR's refusal to recognize the EEC prevented this principle from being totally put into effect; thus, agreements are signed by each country but are discussed beforehand within the Community institutions. However, the situation had recently begun to "thaw," and talks are under way between the EEC and the USSR. (The other Eastern countries have a more open attitude.)

3. With developing countries, relations are more varied, because there are exchanges of goods, technological transfers, and financial aids for development. Moreover, the fact that there are historical ties between some Community countries and some developing countries has led to the maintenance of most favored-nation relations with the latter (the Associated States).

The essential Community decisions in these matters have been of three kinds. To begin with, as specified in the Treaty, a Common Custom Tariff was brought into operation to replace the national tariffs. This was done two years ahead of the initial deadline. Second, the Community played a decisive part in the international discussions aimed at reducing the obstacles to trade and, more particularly, tariff barriers. In this connection, the fact that the Community spoke with a single voice at the Kennedy Round certainly played an important part in its success. Finally, especially during the last few years, a series of trade agreements have been made with a considerable number of nonmember countries.

Three questions arise in connection with these decisions. One that concerns the outside world is whether the attitude adopted reflects a turning in upon itself or an opening up toward the outside world. The others, which concern the Community are: How has the specialization of exports developed and can a real commercial policy be said to exist? And how has the Community balance of payments been equilibrated with the rest of the world?

Opening Up or Turning Inward?

The Community has repeatedly stated that, in conformity with the Treaty, and contrary to various allegations by nonmember countries, the Community's commercial policy is one of an open character. This claim is confirmed by a number of statistical indicators.

Far from leading to a turning inward of the member countries among themselves, the formation of the EEC has been accompanied by an intensification in its relations with nonmember countries: EEC trade with countries outside the EEC (average of exports and imports) between 1958 and 1970 grew at a pace of 9 percent per year, as opposed to the pace of 8 percent for world trade. Therefore, the Community of Six's share of world trade also increased slightly, rising from 17.5 percent in 1958 to 19 percent in 1973. In this, the Community of Six became the top-ranking trading group in the world.[*] This position has obviously become stronger with the enlarging of the Community. In 1975, the EEC accounted for 22 percent of world trade (excluding intra-Community trade). This share is one and a half times that of the United States (14.5 percent), two and half times that of Japan, four times that of Canada, and five times that of the USSR.

Furthermore, examination by a GATT working party of the tariff situation as it would appear if all the Kennedy Round decisions

---

[*] Furthermore, it is to be noted that in total world trade (including trade between the Six), the Community has only regained the position it held before the First World War (32 percent in 1900 and 1913, 21 percent in 1938, and 28 percent in 1968). Also, curiously

were implemented has shown that the Community tariff is the lowest
among the world's great trading powers: for the EEC, the average
level would be 6 percent, as opposed to 7.1 percent for the United
States, 7.6 percent for the United Kingdom, and 9.7 percent for
Japan.[1]

What products have been especially involved in this increase
in trade? The Community, like many industrial countries, is an
importer of many raw materials and of energy; it is an exporter,
essentially, of processed goods. It will be found, however, that the
imports of energy and raw materials have increased less rapidly
than have total imports, for their share of the total has fallen from 47
percent to 37 percent. On the other hand, the share represented by
manufactured goods has increased from 27 percent to 46 percent, while
capital goods have risen from 9 percent to 16 percent. Not only is
the Community of Six not a closed shop but it has played an increased
part in the trade in finished industrial products, which, in principle,
reflects a certain international specialization. As far as exports are
concerned, the increased share of capital goods should be noted,
rising from 33 percent to 42 percent.

Currently, the Community is the world's leading importer of
agricultural produce, raw materials, and energy. It yields first
place to the United States for capital goods, but the percentage of
gross fixed capital formation produced by imported machinery is
much the same.

In exports, the Community's almost exclusive concentration
on manufactured goods (85 percent of total exports, as opposed to
75 percent in the United States) makes it the world's leading supplier.
Thus, for this category of goods, the Common Market countries'
share accounted for around 45 percent of world exports (excluding
intra-Community trade) in 1974. If one takes capital goods alone, the
Community keeps its leading position, but the United States ranks a
close second.

Finally, there are certain changes to be noted in the relative
positions of the trading partners: (1) in exports, the industrialized
countries' share has greatly increased, to the detriment of that of
the developing countries—this growth is particularly high in exports
to the United States and other European countries; and (2) in
imports, the same kind of distortion occurs, but on a far smaller
scale.

_____

enough, the position of the United States has barely changed, whereas
that of the United Kingdom has fallen greatly and that of Japan has
greatly increased.

Specialization

In Chapter 1, the specialization trends in the member countries within the framework of intra-Community trade were discussed. It will be worthwhile to continue that analysis now in considering trade with nonmember countries.

The behavior of the Six exporters may especially be seen on a market which groups most industrialized countries except Japan, and which is constituted by the trade between the EEC (excepting intra-Community trade), the European Free Trade Association (EFTA), and North America. *

The methodological approach is the same as with intra-Community trade and is based on working out the coefficient of predominance for the years 1955 and 1970. [2]

An overall analysis of the developments of 1955-70, dealing with 19 industries and covering 90 percent of total exports, brings to light a marked reduction in the gaps between coefficient values corresponding to each country. In other words, a double movement is revealed: a high concentration of exports of one country in some industries tends to decrease parallel to the growth of other countries' exports in the same industries. One example is items manufactured in metal: in the first case, there is a drop in the coefficient of predominance for Germany, whereas there is a very sharp increase for Italy. This can be explained by the industrial development efforts made by Italy and France. But it should be pointed out that the phenomenon is much less marked than in the case of intra-Community trade. Thus, contrary to what has been observed on the Community market, Italy has managed to make the products of its electrical engineering industries predominate only to a moderate degree. The relative positions of the Six are therefore more fixed on the market of nonmember industrialized countries than on the Community market, which, a priori, is scarcely surprising (see Table 5.1).

Is this gradual specialization of exports well advised? This is a question that should be asked because external trade is not an end in itself but a means of fulfilling its needs at the least cost.

An economic area of the size of the Community is capable of producing almost every industrial product it needs. The only exceptions that stand out at the current time seem to be subsonic long-range aircraft and some highly specialized machinery and equipment. The

---

*This geographic area takes in about 60 percent of EEC exports. (The other industrialized countries receive 6 percent, the developing countries 26 percent, and countries with state-run trade 8 percent.)

TABLE 5.1

Specialization in Trade with Countries outside the Community, 1970

Industries	Germany	France	Italy	Netherlands	Belgium and Luxembourg
Transport equipment	++	+	-	--	=
Metal goods	+	-	+	=	=
Press and publishing	+	+	+	++	--
Machinery, except electrical machinery	+	-	=	--	--
Chemicals	+	=	--	+	-
Electrical machinery	=	-	-	+	--
Wood and furniture	=	-	++	--	-
Textiles	=	=	=	+	+
Rubber	=	=	++	++	--
Iron and steel	=	++	--	=	++
Building material, glass, and so forth	-	=	=	--	++
Nonferrous metals	-	-	--	--	++
Mineral fuels	-	+	++	++	+
Clothing	-	-	+	++	-
Fats	-	--	-	+	--
Leather and shoes	--	+	++	--	--
Paper and cardboard	--	--	--	--	--
Raw materials, except for mineral fuels (other than textile fibers)	--	-	--	++	-
Agriculture and foodstuffs	--	+	=	++	--

++ = k>1.5, high level of specialization.
+ = 1.1<k<1.5, rather high level of specialization.
= = 0.9<k<1.1, average specialization.
- = 0.5<k<0.9, low level of specialization.
-- = k<0.5, insignificant level of specialization.
Source: Compiled by the author.

imports that are strictly necessary, therefore, would include various agricultural and food products, especially those of tropical origin; most raw materials; a large part of its energy; and the various manufactured articles mentioned above.

This "strict necessity" list would cover 60 percent of the total imports in 1969, as compared with 75 percent in 1958. The rest, which reflects world specialization in certain lines of production and a desire for variety among European consumers, rose from 25 percent to 40 percent of the total.

Again, is this specialization—which is reflected both in the kind of imports and in the kind of exports—well advised?

From the economic point of view, it is well advised for the Community to export goods for which the difference between the selling price and the marginal production cost is particularly great. This is true of industries where economies of scale have a great effect and where the internal market is large. It is also true for new products that yield the producer a kind of "novelty rent" for at least as long as competitors do not appear on the market (theory of product cycle); and of products for which the market increases rapidly (because it is possible to saturate the production capacity in a short time and, thus, rapidly pay off investments and research expenses).

Defining a real commercial policy must be the corollary of a foreign policy, particularly when the development of links with certain countries is sought, and an industrial policy, through which it seeks to promote the development of specific production lines or to organize a decrease in others. The several dozen trade agreements concluded with nonmember countries do not yet reflect any real foreign policy, and the granting of generalized preferences was not sufficiently geared to an industrial policy that had been defined in its sectoral aspects.

In actual fact, at the beginning, the absence of foreign policy discussions at Community level led to the signing of trade agreements as the opportunity arose, primarily under the influence of the general desire to take an open attitude toward the outside world. This is a state of things that the European Parliament has often regretted.

It was not until September 1972 that an overall conception was worked out. Even so, it covered only one region of the world—the Mediterranean area—but it did at least reflect priorities in the establishment of relations with nonmember countries. The guiding line of this conception was that agreements should be drawn up with a comprehensive and balanced approach; this included, therefore, a progressive reduction in the obstacles to trade; actions of economic, technical, and financial cooperation; and measures in favor of immigrant labor.

Moreover, the lack of any definition of industrial policy, in its sectoral aspects, has also precluded the existence of any reference

framework for the purpose of trade negotiations, and the risk is that
the compromises arrived at may be dictated more by short-term
problems than by developments that would be desirable in the medium
term. This is all the more regrettable since one of the lessons learned
from the first few years of the EEC was that most of the fears
expressed in the different sectors proved to be exaggerated and that,
in general, the adjustments have been easier than was expected—so
much so that safeguard measures have usually been excessive and
have unecessarily slowed down the beneficial adjustments.

Thus, it would still be a little exaggerated to speak here about
the Community as the leading trading power in the world. However,
it should be pointed out that the Community provides the most important statistical line in the foreign trade yearbooks. It only has to
transform this statistical predominance into an economic reality
through a real foreign policy.

Community's Balance of Payments

The Community of Six's balance of payments in goods and
services with the rest of the world was consistently in credit throughout the 1958-73 period. It amounted in all to about $63 billion. Where
does this balance come from, and what use has been made of it?

Most of the positive balance results from the movements of
goods ($51 billion): the Community of Six exported far more to
nonmember countries than it imported. If this surplus was small
during the three years 1962-64 (almost to the point of disappearing
in 1963 because of the enormous deterioration in Italy's balance),
it started its upward movement again in the following years. This
balance is primarily due to Germany. The surplus shown in services
($12 billion) has tended to drop off over the years; it even went into
deficit in 1970 because of the dramatic shift in the tourist trade
balance. This surplus in services for the Community is the total of
a deficit for Germany and a surplus for each of the other countries.

What use has been made of this balance? It is divided under
the following three headings:

The first heading is private and, more especially, public uni-
lateral transfers. The accumulated total of these is $29 billion. It
consists primarily of public aid to developing countries.

The second heading consists of nonmonetary movements of capital. Against a total foreign investment in the Community of $48 billion,
the Community investments in the rest of the world amount to $60
billion. The last heading is the gold and foreign currency balances,
which are seen to have increased by about $30 billion between 1958
and 1973, (the total of these various uses exceeds the Community's
resources by about $8 billion, which is the total under "errors and
omissions" in the Community's balance of payments).

The last heading is the gold and foreign currency balances, which are seen to have increased by about $30 billion between 1958 and 1973. (The total of these various uses exceeds the Community's resources by about $8 billion, which is the total under "errors and omissions" in the Community's balance of payments.)

These various headings, which will be commented on in the following sections, are large in absolute value and modest in relative value; the first and third headings each represent around 5 percent of cumulated GNP for that period, with the two accounts of the second heading representing 0.7 percent and 1.2 percent, respectively.

However, there has been considerable change in the situation since 1973 due both to the widening of the Community and to the oil crisis. In fact, almost all the countries show a deficit in their trade balances, some a moderate deficit and the United Kingdom a very large one. The Benelux balance differs from one year to the next; only Germany consistently shows a surplus, but even if this used to make up for the deficit of its five partners, it can no longer equilibrate the trade balance of the Nine, given the huge British deficit. Between 1967 and 1973, the Community of Six's surplus fluctuated between about $1 billion and $2 billion. With the Community of Nine, there has been an average yearly deficit of $3 billion. Moreover, the increase in the price of oil has brought about a major deterioration in the Community trade balance since 1974 (with Germany, however, still showing a surplus).

AID TO THE DEVELOPING COUNTRIES

The notion of aid to developing countries is not a clear one. Table 5.2 is based on the definitions laid down by the Organization for Economic Cooperation and Development (OECD) Development Assistance Committee.[3] It can be seen that, for the period 1958-69, the total aid supplied by the Community reached almost $37 billion, divided almost equally between public aid and private aid. (This figure is significantly higher than the figure for the balance of payments mentioned above, because it includes grants and loans—private aid, in particular, includes mainly loans.)

During this period, the ratio $\frac{\text{total aid}}{\text{GNP}}$ first decreased (from 1.44 in 1958 to 0.89 in 1965) and then increased (to 1.22 in 1969). Public aid dropped from 0.80 in 1958 to 0.40 in 1964, then remained more or less stationary.

If the aid is broken down according to the receiving regions, Africa clearly received the largest share, followed by Asia and America. But such an overview oversimplifies things, because

TABLE 5.2

EEC Aid to Developing Countries, 1958-69
(in billions of dollars)

Form of Aid	EEC	Germany	France	Italy	Netherlands	Belgium
Public aid:	19.0	5.5	10.4	1.2	1.0	0.9
Bilateral	16.6	4.4	9.8	0.9	0.8	0.6
Multilateral	2.4	1.1	0.6	0.3	0.2	0.3
Private aid	17.9	5.6	6.3	3.2	1.1	1.7
Total	36.9	11.1	16.7	4.4	2.1	2.6
In Percent of GNP						
Total	1.19	0.92	1.54	0.69	1.16	1.25
Public Aid	0.61	0.46	0.96	0.19	0.55	0.43

Source: OECD, Development Assistance Committe.

actually Africa's share has been continually on the decrease, year
by year, falling from more than half at the beginning of this period
to less than a third by the end, the aid having been shifted to Asia and,
to a lesser degree, to South America. This shift is due to the redirecting of France's and Belgium's aid, 80 percent of which was
originally concentrated in Africa.

A large part of the action was taken by the member countries
themselves, in the form of financial and technical cooperation. As
stated in a Commission memorandum on a Community policy of development cooperation (1971):

If, in 1969* all the countries reached the target of
transferring to the developing countries at least 1%
of their GNP, including public and private flows, the
same cannot be said of the target of 0.7% in the form
of public flows. On this point there are quite considerable differences between the member countries.
There are also rather considerable differences in the
division of the bilateral public aid between grants and
loans and in the terms on which the public loans are
granted. The volume of the aid, too, has shown quite
considerable variations from year to year.

These divergencies are a reflection, firstly, of
allowance made by the member countries for internal
pressure of a historical, economic and political kind
which are often different, and secondly, of the absence
of any sufficient coordination between the bilateral
policies.

Community action takes three forms: a convention with certain
countries (African, Caribbean, and Pacific countries [ACP]); the
setting up of the generalized preferences scheme (GPS); and the establishing of special ties with the Mediterranean countries.

The association of some developing countries with the Community
has slowly developed, both in the number of countries concerned and
the means of action undertaken. In a first stage, the association with
the African states and Madagascar has gradually assumed a character
going far beyond the simple implementation of technical and financial
aid and measures of trade preference. It thus expresses a real political option of developing special relations between Europe and Africa

---

* The information available for the years following shows
a falling off in some countries' financial contribution by comparison
with 1969.

south of the Sahara. The most apparent financial aspect is to be found in the successive appropriations for the European Development Fund (EDF). The first EDF, decided on by the Rome Treaty, had resources of 580 million ua. The second EDF was created under the first Yaoundé Convention in 1963, and its resources were 730 million ua, plus a further 70 million ua made available by the European Investment Bank. The third EDF was set up under the second Yaoundé Convention in 1970, and its resources were 900 million ua, plus a further 100 million ua from the EIB. In the past few years, the annual expenditure has been at the rate of about 190 million ua, as compared with the national product of the countries aided, which is around 8 billion ua. With the signing of the Lomé Convention on February 28, 1975, a new stage was undertaken in the Community Development Aid Policy. This new convention increased the number of Associated ACP States to 46 and brought some improvements to the previous conventions by implementing new kinds of aid. The main provisions of this convention are:

1. to set up a system of stabilizing export earnings by introducing a compensation mechanism, which should make it possible to protect the poorer countries from fluctuations in the prices of a certain number of basic products: if exports of one of these products were to drop below a certain preset amount, a compensation fund would advance the difference to the exporting country, and should the situation improve, this country would repay this advance, with the poorest countries being exempt from this repayment obligation;
2. to intensify the EEC financial contributions: the new convention's financial resources have been increased to 3.39 billion ua (2.5 billion ua to the EDF, 390 million ua to the IEB, and 375 million ua for stabilizing export earnings); and
3. to develop industrial and commercial cooperation.

The idea behind the GPS is that all industrialized countries unilaterally grant duty free entry to products coming from each and every developing country. The idea was launched in 1963 by the EEC and later taken up by the United Nations Conference on Trade and Development (UNCTAD) in 1968.

Various application schemes were successively accepted by diverse countries or groups of countries and by the EEC in July 1971 Japan in August 1971, several European countries in 1972, and the United States in 1976. At the outset, duty free entry was limited to certain ceilings, but these ceilings are supposed to be raised each year.

With countries surrounding the Mediterranean, the Community has concluded two kinds of agreements. On one hand, with Greece

and Turkey, Association agreements have been signed. These are
meant to pave the way for these two countries' eventual entry into the
EEC. However, the low level of economic development of these
countries does not allow for their immediate integration and necessitates a transitional period, during which these countries will maintain a degree of protection necessary to enable them to develop their
industry. On the other hand, as seen above, since 1972, a "Mediterranean policy" has been developing, which resulted in the signing
of agreements with various Maghreb countries (Morocco, Algeria,
and Tunisia) and Machrek countries (Egypt, Syria, and Jordan), as
well as with Israel. These agreements go farther than the GPS
agreements, since all industrial exports from these countries (with
a few minor exceptions) enter the EEC duty free and since the EEC
makes a contribution to the economic and social development of these
countries.

   All these measures reflect the same desire to strengthen the
Community's cooperation in the development of the poorer countries.
Nevertheless, they cannot yet be described as a real development
aid policy. There are, in fact, three sources of inconsistency or
difficulty.

   First, there is no overall deliberation at Community level on
the choice of the best instruments for aiding the developing countries, [*]
nor is there any systematic comparison of the commitments or actions
contemplated, either at the national level (especially as regards
technical and financial cooperation) or at the Community level (especially through the commercial policy). This prevents the aid that is
given from having its maximum effect, and it also prevents the views
of the Community in international conferences from carrying their
full weight, a weight that might be attached to them as they come
from the biggest trading partner of the developing countries and the
provider of more than a third of the total aid given by industrialized
countries. The lack of predetermined Community attitudes, put
forward and defended by a single spokesman, has been a major
obstacle for the Community countries in playing any appreciable part
in the successive UNCTAD negotiations. Also, it prevented them from
reaching more concrete conclusions, which could have mitigated the
immense disappointment felt by the participating countries from the
Third World. Though the Community has not suffered any direct
economic damage through this, it has certainly affected the Community's political image this is all the more regrettable since the

---

   [*] This holds true as well for the other industrialized countries
and for various international institutions.

value and effectiveness of a single representative for the Community
have already been proved by the Kennedy Round experience.

Second, maintaining special relations with the Associated States
is difficult to reconcile with the generalized trade preferences. The
choice lies between a progressive loosening of this privileged character of the relations with the ACP countries or maintaining it by giving
them more technical and financial aid.

Third, where the development of the developing countries is
to take place through the diversification of their economies and an
increase in exports of goods that will compete with some Community
products, the situation calls for reorganization of the Community
economic structures. This means that the development aid policy
needs to be closely coordinated with industrial policy and the channelin
of the Social Fund's activities.

AREAS WHERE THE COMMUNITY
HAS FAILED TO ACT

If the Community as such actively intervened in the two fields
examined above, the development of world trade through its participation at the Kennedy Round and aid to developing countries through
the EDF, in contrast, its lack of action stands out sharply—and
deplorably so—in three problem areas: foreign investments, the
international short-term capital market, and the international monetary system. These are three areas that overlap a great deal, because capital movements make it possible to use a national currency
as a reserve currency and, also, because of the role played by the
multinational firms in the movement of floating capital.

Capital Movements and Foreign Investment

Throughout the period 1958-70 as a whole, Community investments in the rest of the world were higher than foreign investments
in the Community by about 16 billion ua. In all, the Community
contributed nearly 0.4 percent of its national product to the financing
of investments on foreign territory. A more detailed look at recent
figures shows that the main recipient countries were the developing
nations and the United States. At the same time, the United States
acts as a main source of investments in the Community. The relation
between the EEC and the developing countries having already been
examined, a more detailed look at the relations with other countries
is now in order. Special attention will be paid to the volume of foreig
investments in Europe and the methods of financing these investments

According to estimations drawn up by the OECD,[4] the total of direct investments made abroad by industrialized countries amounted to around $90 billion in 1966 (in book-entry value), $55 billion for the United States, $16 billion for the United Kingdom, and $3 billion for Canada.* Around two-thirds of these investments were located in the industrialized countries (and a tenth in the United States itself). Some $36 billion went into industry and $26 billion into petroleum.

The values cited here are book values; they should be substantially increased at current market prices. Moreover, it has been estimated that $1 of direct investments in book value corresponds on the average to $2 in turnover. This means that the turnover of American subsidiaries throughout the world might have reached as much as $140 billion in 1969 (of which $60 billion went into processing industries); these figures should be compared with the GNP in the same year of Germany ($186 billion), France ($148 billion), the United Kingdom ($121 billion), Italy ($93 billion) or the total exports of the United States ($40 billion). It is estimated that, in 1972, the turnover of the subsidiaries of foreign firms may have reached nearly $320 billion, or the equivalent of total world trade.

If to all that it is added that multinational companies practice a certain division of labor between their various production units that results in considerable trade, two conclusions may be drawn from these few figures: foreign trade is taking on a new aspect, where trade between the different departments of large companies is being added to the trade between countries,[†] and the conquest of foreign markets is being carried out more and more from within these markets, by setting up factories on the very territory to be supplied.

---

* These figures do not include the minority controls. According to Yernon, the real balances controlled by American firms abroad should run about twice this amount.

† Thus:

One of the most important consequences of the growth of multinational companies is the increasing share of world trade represented by their internal transactions.

A recent study of the American Department of Commerce, dealing with the 320 American companies which handled more than a third of all U.S. exports in 1965, showed that $4.4 billion (52%) of the $8.5 billion in exports handled by these companies went through American foreign-based subsidiaries. Out of this total, 48% in fact went to independent foreign buyers, 29% to subsidiaries for further processing and 3% represented

Between 1960 and 1969, the value of American investments in Europe was multiplied by 3.3 (rising from $6.6 billion to $21.6 billion), while U.S. exports to Europe were only multiplied by 2.1.

In the Community of Six, the increase in the value of American investments has been observed since 1950. Between 1958 and 1959, the book value increased threefold. But the phenomenon picked up speed thereafter, because over a following eight-year period, the multiplier was four. The formation of the Common Market—and the prospect of a common customs tariff—prompted American companies to settle in on this large market being formed. Since 1967, however, the pace has been slowing.[*]

This book value of the European fixed assets in the hands of Americans still only accounts for a modest fraction of the stock of capital of the Community's industry, but this fraction has grown substantially since 1958. The ratio of procurement costs of the American subsidiaries to the total amount of gross fixed capital formation has increased considerably: for the EEC, it rose from 2.2 percent in 1957 to 4.5 percent in 1965.[5]

Foreign investments in the economy of the member countries currently fluctuate around 15 percent: in percent of turnover, it stands at 9 percent in the United Kingdom, 10 percent in France, 15 percent in The Netherlands, 33 percent in Belgium; in percent of share-holding interests in companies, it is 14 percent in Italy and 18 percent in Germany.[6]

Furthermore, the intensity of this investment varies greatly from industry to industry: thus, in percentage of sales of European firms, the sales of European-based American subsidiaries only represented 1.4 percent for paper products and 2.9 percent for food-stuffs, but rose as high as 7 percent for chemical products, 10 percent to 11 percent for mechanical and electrical engineering, 13 percent for tires, and 15 percent for motor-driven vehicles (and, as we have seen, two-thirds for computers).[7]

---

capital goods brought from the United States by these subsidiaries (the 2% remaining went to subsidiaries under an unnamed heading) ("The Growth and Spread of Multi-national Companies." The Economist Intelligence Unit, Q.E.R. special no. 5, rev. ed. 1971).

[*] Meanwhile, the share of the EEC in American foreign investments rose from 5.4 percent in 1950, to 7.0 percent in 1958, and then to 14.9 percent in 1970.

The financing of foreign investments brings to light a clear difference between European and American behavior:

1. The growth in Europe of indebtedness in the United States has been greater than that of American indebtedness in Europe, but this disparity only shows up for short-term indebtedness (mainly, American debts held by European banks). However, for long-term indebtedness, the rate of growth is an inverse one.
2. The United States makes massive direct investments in Europe, whereas Europeans, above all, buy securities (stocks and bonds).
3. The general effect is as if Europe were lending on short term and the United States on long term, thus presenting a case of a phenomenon of transformation.*

More precisely, we notice that, except from 1950 to 1962, funds coming from the United States have never provided more than a quarter of the financing of European-based American films. Amortization and profits contribute at the most 40 percent to this financing, and funds from outside the United States, that is, funds mainly found on the European market, up to another 40 percent.

If we exclude amortization and thus think in terms of net investment, the financing of the latter would be provided by: reinvested profits—20 percent to 25 percent; funds coming from the United States—more than 50 percent; and funds from outside the United States—more than 50 percent.

Furthermore, the total reinvestment of profits would make possible a growth rate of the book value equal to the rate of return, that is, 8 percent to 10 percent over the last few years (Survey of Current Business). Yet the average rate during the 1963-69 period was around 12 percent. Thus, the process could have almost been maintained by itself.†

The previous information may be summed up in this manner:

1. The direct investments of nonmember countries (essentially American) in the Community have greatly increased, year by year, for the last 20 years; they picked up speed after the formation of the Common Market.

---

* Indeed, this is the interpretation of some American writers, particularly Kindleberger.

† On a world scale, capital outflows corresponding to American direct investments abroad rose to $42 billion between 1950 and 1971, whereas the corresponding repatriated profits rose to $77 billion.

2. The fraction of the Community's production capacities controlled in this way from abroad is still modest on the whole, but it is becoming considerable in some industries.

3. The financing of these investments is, for the most part, provided by European saving and, in part, by reinvested profits.

Such a situation has both its advantages and drawbacks, which have been clearly summed up in a report by a group of experts from the OECD:

> Multinational firms play an important and positive role in the transfer of financial resources, technology and business management techniques from developed countries to the Less Developed Countries. In the host countries, they create new jobs, increase the vocational skills of labor, improve industrial structures, often contribute to regional development and generally stimulate economic growth. More generally, they contribute to a better use of productive resources, to an improvement in efficiency and to economic growth in the world. They constitute a predominant factor of a dynamic world economy and an important factor in the development of certain regions and certain countries.
>
> However, the Group is aware of the concerns to which multinationals have often given birth. These concerns have various causes such as the relative economic power these firms have in comparison with the States taken individually, as well as the economic dependence of some industries in regard to decisions made abroad. More specifically, there has been some anxiety about the effects on production or employment which may result from the multinational firms' more rapid possibilities of adaptation to changes in circumstances, or then again, the dominant positions they may acquire. Other questions have been raised about the extra-territoriality or the application of the laws and regulations of the parent company's country to the activities of its foreign subsidiaries; the relationship between the transfer price and various national provisions or policies like taxation; the influence multinationals may exercise over short-term capital movements through their financial operation and the management of their funds.
>
> These same concerns have been summed up in vigorous terms in Georges Ball's question: "How can

a national government work out an economic plan with
any certainty if a board of directors meeting some
5,000 miles away is in a position, by changing its purchasing and production policy, to influence decisively
the country's economic life?" The same question can
be asked substituting "Community" for "National
Government."[8]

The development of multinational firms, and more particularly
the interest they have increasingly shown, for ten years or more, in
the countries of Europe, have substantially modified the basic data
of some of the Community's economic problems and the scope of
some of its measures. What is the use of minor adjustments to
customs tariffs, which may raise or reduce import prices by 2 percent or 3 percent, when the foreign subsidiaries of American
companies have a turnover that is six times the total exports from
the United States (and the same will shortly apply to Japanese firms)?
What is the point of liberalizing public contracts for the benefit of
big European firms that sell half or two-thirds of their products outside the Community, either by exporting them or by manufacturing
them through subsidiaries in nonmember countries? What is the
value of aid to a branch of industry doing a total business of 20
million or 30 million ua in the face of firms with an annual turnover
of 1 billion ua or more and a gross annual profit of around 100
million ua a year? What can be the effect of a monetary policy aimed
at making a change by 10 percent, that is to say, by 15 billion ua
in the Community's monetary stock, when the world has a stock
of around 50 billion ua, a large part of which can be set in motion
at very short notice, largely by the decisions of finance departments
in the multinational companies? (See Table 5.3.)
     Examination of the problems posed by the appearance of these
companies on the European scene, with decision-making centers of
such importance located outside the confines of Europe, has remained
taboo. It was not until July 1972, when the Rey report was laid on
the table in the OECD that the question was raised in all its magnitude
in any official body, and then only briefly, as is shown by the question
given above in full. This is a field where the delay between the problem's first appearance and the decision to tackle it has been particularly great.
     However, a few sporadic attempts have been made. In particular,
the French government has asked that the problem be discussed,
first by the Medium-Term Economic Policy Committee and, then,
by the ad hoc Industrial Questions Working Party. For its part, the
Commission had worked out a program to gather information on the
problem. These attempts ran up against the indifference or opposition

TABLE 5.3

Direct Foreign Investment of the EEC, Japan, Canada,
Switzerland, the United States, and Other Countries in 1969

	Investments in the United States in 1969			American Investments in Other Countries	
	In Value (Total in 10^9)	Percent	In Number of Firms	In 10^9	In Dollars per Capita in 1971
Netherlands	2	16.6	19	1.2	127
Germany	0.6	5.2	50	4.3	85
France	0.3	2.7	21	2.1	59
B.L.E.U.	0.3	2.6	10	1.2	181
United Kingdom	3.5	29.6	101	7.2	161
Canada	2.8	24.0	113	21.1	—
Switzerland	1.4	11.8	17	1.6	—
Japan	0.2	1.5	12	32.3	—
Other countries	0.7	6.0	31	—	—
Total	11.8	100.0	374	71.0	

Sources: for value: Survey of Current Business; for number: J. Daniels, Recent Foreign Direct Investment in the United States (New York: Praeger, 1971).

of the member countries, several of which thought that the free movement of long-term capital and the freedom of establishment were a part of the normal economic relations between the Community and nonmember countries and that governments should not intervene in these. When one looks at Table 5.3 and sees the compared volume of American investments in some countries and these countries' investments in the United States, the firmness of the Dutch attitude on this point becomes understandable. For Germany, it was more than a question of doctrinal position.

The problem of American (and Japanese) investments in the Community has thus been left largely untouched at the Community level, which makes it possible for foreign firms to cleverly play one government off against another in order to obtain favors, tax-wise or otherwise, when they plan to set up a subsidiary in a region with employment problems.

International Short-Term Capital Market

Despite the conditions laid down in the Treaty, the Community has not yet managed to harmonize national regulations sufficiently to form a Community capital market. But the needs proved stronger than the resistance of the national administrations; the Community's economic agents played a considerable role in an international market that was almost spontaneously formed, the Eurodollar mar-ket.[*]

After rather slow beginnings, this market has mushroomed astonishingly over the last few years, with a growth rate of more than 30 percent per annum (more than 50 percent in 1969).

The special characteristic of this market is that, unlike transactions in national currencies, Eurodollar transactions are not subject to the control of any public monetary institution. Of course, various central banks have imposed certain rules on the commercial banks in their countries, but only on a modest scale, if only not to put them in an unfavorable position in relation to other countries' banks.

The formation of this market has certainly proved advantageous to commercial banks, for it has given them great flexibility in the

---

[*] According to the International Bank of Settlements, Euro-dollars are dollars acquired by banks located outside the United States (including foreign branches of American banks) and loaned to final borrowers, either directly in dollars or after being converted into another currency, sometimes by calling in an intermediary.

use of their funds by enabling them to profit from the differences
in return, however small, from one place to another. The effect
is the same for big firms, which have heavy reserves on which they
try to earn the highest return; this is particularly true of multinationals, which, because of their subsidiaries, are well placed to
rapidly compute the advantages of investing in various spots.

However, it must not be forgotten that this is essentially a
short-term market, and, thus, does not make a substantial contribution to the total investment of the countries concerned. It may
make the operations of some economic agents easier, but, to a
large degree, what one earns, another loses, and the net contribution
to the whole group is probably modest.

Moreover, such a market can be a serious disturbing factor
in economic life to the extent that, since it is not controlled, it may
counteract the states' monetary policies. As a specialist in this
field, Otto Emminger says:

> However, from the standpoint of the stability of the
> international monetary system, the negative aspects
> override the positive ones.
> What is the good of standardizing the different
> positions of national liquidity and of short-term interest
> rates if it is very often necessary to do the opposite.
> It is undeniable that stabilization policies and
> adjustments of desequilibria in the balance of payments
> frequently make it necessary to put into effect national
> liquidity and interest rate policies which may differ
> from one country to the next or even conflict.
> Thus, the enormous pool of international liqui-
> dity, which is ready in an instant to flow in here or there,
> more often threatens national stabilization policies and
> adjustments policies than it buttresses them.
> This is why these short-term capital movements
> probably more often have a destabilizing rather than a
> stabilizing impact: they reinforce the real deficit
> "below the line" of the balance of payments, anaes-
> thetize the automatic adjustment mechanism and are
> likely to transform a small scale speculative flurry into
> a major exchange crisis.
> The simple "recycling" of short-term funds from
> one central bank to another does not seem to be a solu-
> tion to the real problem at hand. Thus, the Euromarket
> has made monetary management much more difficult
> and complicated at the national level as well as the
> international.

In fact, one of the main problems of European
monetary policy is to know if and how, with such a
mass of international liquidity prowling at their door,
the central banks will be able to maintain their control
of the liquidity positions of the commercial banks and
of the volume of national money supply.
Some central banks have drawn the conclusion
from this situation that the variations in the net foreign
position of their banks is an important factor in the
internal liquidity of the economy.[9]

In the previous chapter, it was shown that, for the last few
years, the Commission has repeatedly drawn attention to the fact
that it was necessary to organize, at the Community level, a certain
control of the Euromarket "monster" (as the Economist called it).
It was only in March 1972 that the Council took a first decision
(largely one of principle). It took the rebirth of monetary crises
and an increase in the amount of dollars the Bundesbank was forced
to buy every time there was speculation on the deutsche mark before
the Council recognized, in March 1973, the necessity of putting
real measures into effect.

Overhauling the World Monetary Order

The first cracks in the 30-year-old Brctton Woods edifice
were seen by the specialists a decade or more ago.
The basic faults in the dominant currency standard were
summarized with great deal of clarity by Robert Triffin:

1. As long as the dominant currency is still convertible into
gold, the balance-of-payments discipline can operate, but with
convertibility crises that will shake the economic foundations of
all countries.
2. If this dominant currency should become inconvertible,
either de jure or de facto, it will become an uncontrollable instrument of world inflation, for it will oblige the other countries to
provide unlimited finance for the external deficit of the dominant
currency country. The system amounts to a positive subsidization
by the other countries.

In addition to this, but not independent of it, is the progressive
development of an international money market (and, on a more
modest scale, a finance market) that, by comparison with the national
money markets, has the peculiarity of not being under the control
of any public authority.

The Community has suffered these upsets and anomalies in several different ways. In the first place, the "droits de seignieuriage"[*] have cost in 15 years more than $20 billion, which could have been applied to much better effect internally or in helping the developing nations.

Much more important, however, are the obstacles this monetary system puts in the way of policies of short-term economic control. Transmission through the intermediary of the Eurodollar market results in a certain subjection of the European central bank rates to the Eurodollar rate, which is itself influenced by the Federal Reserve rate. It is quite generally appreciated that the Eurodollar is an inflationary factor, tending to have a destabilizing effect on European economies; and the ill effects from which these economies suffer are essentially attributable to the disparity of scale between the American economy and the separate economies of Europe. The way out, of course, lies either in the formation of a true monetary union or in a reorganization of the international monetary system.

It is the very success of the Common Market, in terms of efficiency of production, that has given so much importance to the international problems with which it is faced. By the fact that it has become the world's foremost trading power, its responsibilities have increased, not only in world trade but also vis-a-vis the developing countries. It is also an area of prosperity, and thus has attracted onto its soil the subsidiaries of foreign companies. The Treaty, which was primarily drawn up to organize the functioning of the Common Market, provided no explicit answer to these questions, except in introducing the Common Customs Tariff and the principle that, after the initial transition period, there should be a common commercial policy. The fact that most of these external economic problems are closely linked with foreign policy explains why progress in dealing with them has been much slower, and hence, more modest in scope, than the progress made in effecting the internal changes in the Community itself. The fact remains that the continued fashioning of Europe will very quickly be blocked if these new problems are not tackled and resolved with a degree of care commensurate with their importance.

---

[*]In the Middle Ages each <u>seigneur</u> had the right to mint his own coins.

NOTES

1. GATT, Analyse des tarifs (1971).

2. Detailed figures are given in the EEC report, "Rapport Retro" mimeographed (1972).

3. OECD, Development Assistance Committee, "Statistics group" (Paris: OECD, 1971).

4. Cited in "The Growth and Spread of Multinational Companies," The Economist Intelligence Unit, Q.E.R. special no. 5, rev. Ed. (1971).

5. DATAR, Les Firmes Multinationales, collection "Travaux et recherches de prospective," no. 34.

6. See EEC "Les entreprises multinationales dans le contexte des reglements communautaires", (1973).

7. See M. H. Dunning, Studies in International Investment (London: Allen and Unwin, 1970), quoted in DATAR, op. cit.

8. OECD, Rey Report.

9. Various authors, L'Eurodollar, series "Perspectives de l'économique" (Paris: Calmann-Levy, 1971).

6

TOMORROW'S TASKS

NEW PROBLEMS

Twenty years ago, when the Treaty of Rome was signed, the economic and social future of the Community countries were matters both of hope and of anxiety.

The hopes were expressed with particular vigor by most economists, many politicians, and a number of business and union leaders. Two points were specially emphasized. First, people looked for a profound change in production structures, which would enable the improvements in efficiency arising through greater specialization and economies of scale to be exploited to the full. Second, they expected that a real European economic entity could be very quickly constituted and that, inside it, ideas would crystallize about the European society of tomorrow and the role Europe should play in the world.

The anxieties were felt more especially by various people in direct everyday contact with the realities. Many business leaders feared that the opening of the frontiers to the passage of goods and the free movement of capital and freedom of establishment might result in unduly abrupt changes in the supply of particular types of goods and thus bring about the need for a thorough structural reorganization of firms. Unions feared that the same factors might lead to large areas of unemployment and necessitate the retraining and resettlement of large numbers of workers in conditions that would be all the more difficult because preparations would not have been made far enough in advance. And the administrations feared that the reduction of national powers might lead to difficulties in managing economic trends and in working toward greater harmony between different regions.

Experience has shown that both the good and the bad expectations were exaggerated. Setting up the Common Market has not caused the upheavals that some people feared; though there have been appreciable shifts in many trade flows, no real disturbances have occurred, except in a few instances where ill effects were, in any case, mitigated by the application of safeguard measures. It has been possible to continue controlling economic trends at least as effectively as in previous years, and there has been no increase in the regional imbalances. At the same time, economic growth has continued at a rapid pace, making possible a greater improvement in standards of living than in any of the other Western countries, and the opening of the frontiers has put a much greater variety of supplies at the disposal of the consumer.

Industrial reorganization across the frontiers, however, is still on a small scale, and for a number of industrial goods, it is not possible to regard the market as having been unified at all. Preparation for the future, through a joint research policy and harmonized regional concepts, is still in its early stages; the Monetary Union is advancing only slowly, and now and then goes into reverse. The common attitudes to the major international problems—whether they concern the creation of a new world monetary system or contributing to the development of the underdeveloped countries—are still in the drafting stage. The task is far from finished.

Chronologically, the first years of the Common Market were marked by many achievements, both in the fields of legislation and regulation and in those of transformation of production structures and the broadening of intra-Community trade. After this came a period in which the adoption of decisions of immediate application, which characterized the earlier years, was largely superseded by declarations of intent. There were capable a priori of producing profound changes in the economic and social development of the Community, but they could not have any such effect until they were followed by concrete decisions, which were often a long time in coming.

Why, then, has there been this temporary slackening in the Community's activity? In the early years, the main concern was to clear away the obstacles that had been created artificially by the individual countries to hamper trade between the nations. For the most part, the precise instructions contained in the Treaty have been carried out, so that the end of the initial transition period was officially declared on July 1, 1968.

In the following years, the task became more difficult. The barriers had indeed been thrown down, but now it was a question of working out the common policies. A large economic area had been created as a first step, and the Community's assignment was to find a joint definition of the objectives of the new actions to be taken.

The Treaty of Rome was based on a clearly expressed vision of how the economy would function ten years later. The final state of things at the end of the transition period was to be characterized by the free circulation of goods, capital, and people, with economic activity continuing in an institutional framework of which the main lines were laid down in the Treaty. This concept was influenced by the priority given to the problems that were being faced 20 years ago, and by certain definitive economic concepts.

In the early 1950s, the major common concerns in the various countries centered on three themes: to raise the standard of living; to break down the divisions between the different economies; and to strengthen the European potential in a climate of Cold War.

Increased production, considered as the top priority of economic policy; the opening of the borders and the formation of a large European market; and the Atlantic Alliance were the three ideas that underlay national actions.

Within a quarter of a century, the answers formed to these concerns have been so successful, particularly as regards increased production and the formation of a large European market, that the old problems have dramatically changed: the old ones have faded away but new ones loom ahead.

The open debate on the ends of growth—indeed, even the usefulness of growth—is far from over. Even if the ideas of zero growth have no chance of winning, the fetishism of quantitative growth at all costs has been destroyed. Even if the words change—use of the "fruits of growth," "quality of life," "environment," and so forth—the basic problem remains: For what are we working? And if in these last few years "living conditions" have been the major topic of discussion, in the coming years, "working conditions" will once again be the center of discussion.

On the other hand, the external circumstances have changed greatly; the hostile bipolarity of the world of 1957 has given way to a multipolarity, which has every chance of increasing in the coming years. First, the position occupied by multinational firms is rapidly growing larger: the foreign-based production of multinationals is increasing by about 10 percent per year, or twice as fast as world GNP and one and one-half times faster than international trade. Second, the wish to open outward is a fairly general one, even if the musty smell of protectionism can be found here and there. This holds true not only for the Western world but, also, and especially very recently, for the relations between the Western countries and the countries of the East. Third, the gap is widening between the rich nations and the developing countries. Not only has the aid to these countries failed to be increased as it should, but the most severe doubts have been raised as to the effectiveness of the forms this aid

has taken for the last 20 years. Last, the international monetary
system, as pointed out above, steadily deteriorated, until finally it
fell to pieces at the time of the Nixon decisions in August 1971.

Therefore, the traditional distinction drawn between internal
and external problems has largely become obsolete and will become
even more so, because of:

1. an increased resolve, on the part of all the countries, to
open outward. Even State Socialist countries, which showed the most
reserve on this point, are evolving and are trying to make use of the
intensification of foreign economic relations with Western countries
to help develop their economies.

2. extraordinary technological transformations of the means
of transport (a substantial reduction in the cost of mass intercontinental
transports resulting from bigger ships and the reduced passenger
transport time due to supersonic aircraft) and, above all, telecommunications (particularly spatial).

3. the development of multinational firms, which, with their
economic weight and their international commercial and financial
strategies, seriously call into question how far-reaching decisions
made at the national level may be.

4. enormous differences in the power of various countries,
which raises the question of how much autonomy medium-sized or
small countries retain in choosing their economic and social development.

The change in the international context alters the comparative
urgency of the problems to be dealt with and demands a series of
major accomplishments from the Community that require sustained
political resolve.

A FULL PROGRAM

Given this new world backdrop, what are the essential tasks
awaiting the Community in the coming years? They may be grouped
under five main themes, listed in ascending order of difficulty:

1. completing the formation of a real common market, where
the "four freedoms" would be totally respected: the freedom of movement for persons, for goods, for capital, and for undertakings;

2. working out real structural policies—these only exist to a
certain degree for agriculture and, to a lesser degree, for the iron
and steel industry and for coal mining; they must be worked out for
all industries where the need is felt;

3. a true harmonization of macroeconomic policies, making possible the complete achievement of the Economic and Monetary Union;

4. defining and putting into effect a wide intra-Community solidarity above and beyond national borders; and

5. adopting a single Community stand vis-a-vis the rest of the world, whether it be the industrialized world or the developing countries.

Completing the Common Market and the policy of production structures has as its purpose to obtain the maximum efficiency that might be obtained from the pooling of the economies of the nine member countries. It consists of extending and improving those measures already taken.

Harmonizing macroeconomic policies goes further. First of all, the general economic conditions must be created to enable the Common Market to function smoothly by setting up a single monetary area. The lines along which the Community wishes to pursue its medium- and long-term development must be defined jointly. What form of society does Europe wish to have in 10 years, in 30 years? What measures should be taken today to attain these objectives?

Community solidarity would be the extension to all nine countries of a concept that has been developing little by little at the national level, and which has shown up in such things as the national budget for social expenditure, in measures aiming at correcting regional imbalances, and in such sectoral support policies as the agricultural policy.

Finally, in a world where each of the partners has its own identity, policy, and problems, it is essential that the Community define a single stand for itself, which will enable it to help introduce more order and justice into international relations.

These five themes are obviously not independent of each other, and all have recourse, in part, to the same instruments: thus, regional policy aims at ensuring simultaneously a better use of production factors and more social justice between regions. Industrial reorganization aims at increasing efficiency but must take into account social aspects (such as working conditions), regional aspects, and foreign policy. Therefore, after having examined these five themes in succession, we will proffer a synthesis to underline the need for joint long-range planning and institutional reforms, which would make it possible to speed up and improve the decision-making and decision-implementing process.

Goal: Completion of the Common Market

The first task that comes to mind is obviously the completion of the Common Market: it is imperative, at least as much for psychological reasons as for economic ones, that goods may move freely without any formality throughout Community territory. Thus, it is important that efforts to harmonize customs and technical regulations be continued unremittingly, as well as efforts to draw up a common law of corporations.

However, the two decisive tasks are to open public tenders, which is closely tied to changing industrial structures (see below), and to draw tax systems closer together.

Although all the countries have adopted the value added tax, there is still a long way to go before the rates are equal and the other taxes are harmonized. In order to avoid double taxation, the system of taxing at the place of destination was adopted.

Harmonizing structures should not pose very large-scale problems (even if some adjustments are rather difficult), yet equalizing the tax rate between countries raises enormous economic and political difficulties. There may be an appreciable change in the taxation on certain products in some countries. (In Chapter 2, for example, it was seen that the purchase tax on cars varied greatly from country to country.) This would not change the comparative position of the producers in the various countries, since they are presently on equal grounds in each national market (every car purchased in France pays 33 percent in taxes), but it might alter the conditions of competition between producers of substitutable products if the relative taxes on these products were greatly modified; therefore, some progressive harmonization may be necessary.

Far more serious problems are posed by the political difficulties. Harmonizing the indirect tax rates, which are currently very different, would entail, at least for some countries, a true revolution in the relation between direct and indirect taxes. For example, aligning the proportion of direct taxes on the level currently applied in Germany would bring a 20 percent drop in the rate in The Netherlands, but more than a 50 percent increase in France. Such changes would bring about serious difficulties for the national governments. Moreover, equalizing indirect taxes would transfer to direct taxes alone the disparities in the rate of tax levies (taxes/GNP) that may exist between countries due to different conceptions on the scope (and use) of public expenditure. If we add that trying to establish a certain tax neutrality regarding the sites where firms choose to set up operations argues in favor of an alignment of taxes on corporate profits, it becomes clear that taxes on family incomes alone will provide the resources for adaptations.*

It is obvious that the difficulties are of such scope that a total harmonization of rates may not be considered for the near future. Nevertheless, in face of the utility to the Common Market of eliminating the tax cordon at the borders, it may be wondered if it is necessary to go so far as a complete equalization of rates between countries. The Commission has made a step in that direction in writing: "The harmonization of rates, which does not need to lead to their total standardization in all cases, must be carried out in several phases."[1]

Thus, the wisest solution might be sought in these ways: considerable alignment of rates, thanks to an alignment of tax structures (the ratio direct tax/indirect tax); and deciding to eliminate the system of deducting charges and then reapplying them at border crossings, as soon as the disparities between VAT rates drops below a certain level.

This level should be determined by carefully comparing the respective drawbacks of retaining the tax cordon at the borders and of a free movement of goods between countries having a few tax differences.

Development of a Structural Policy

As seen in Chapter 2, the reorganizations in the productive apparatus are carried out, with a few exceptions, without any overall conception, so that the Community has not derived all the advantages that could be expected from the economies of scale in various industries. Furthermore, many reorganizations are carried out at the national level, thus increasing the tendency to place public tenders with national suppliers first. Finally, the Community has not used its overall economic potential to embark, in a coordinated and efficient way, upon large technological operations.

If competition policy, the formation of a favorable legal framework, and the opening of public tenders are likely to have favorable effects, measures that are more positive and which show more resolve must be taken in three major fields: (1) industries of high capital

---

* Furthermore, it may be pointed out that, if between Germany and France the direct tax ratio is 46/28, the ratio of family income tax is 42/18; France's aligning on Germany would lead to a doubling.

intensity, where the excessive investment represents a serious loss for the whole economy; (2) troubled industries, needing reorganization, when coordination between countries seems necessary; and (3) operations where working at the Community level would make major economies possible, or would even be the only efficient level (large projects).

In the first kind of industries, the cost of investments is very high compared with the added value, and a unit of production has a large economic size in relation to the annual growth of the market. The Community's total production capacity advances by jumps, and it is important that there be a maximum of coordination among the investment decisions of the various firms (a coordination aimed at preventing great and lasting surpluses in capacity). This problem exists in iron and steel, some branches of chemistry, oil refineries, and so on.

This coordination of investments, of course, could be left in the hands of the firms. But besides being difficult, this could be a start down the road to agreements on market sharing and on prices. Thus, some kind of public supervision is needed, which the procedure provided for the ECSC in the Paris Treaty (general objectives and opinions on investments projects) would generalize. (Moreover, the same need for coordination is felt for some public investments.)

When only one firm needs to be reorganized, especially if it is a medium-sized firm, the problem should be handled more on a national level—coming within the jurisdiction of something like the Institut de Développement Industriel (IDI) in France, or the National Enterprise Board in the United Kingdom, or a regional development association.

On the other hand, when, because of rapid developments in technology or in the market, a whole sector is having difficulty, the Community should take care of such cases. National interventions may be inconsistent, and there may be a real race for subsidies. With the intensity of technological changes, the phenomenon observed for agriculture, coal mining, and shipbuilding has every chance of showing up in other industries.

Last—and above all—the need for Community action is being felt in those industries where new solutions to problems may be found by leaving the national level and going to the Community level. This is true particularly in those industries where the economic size of the undertaking is almost on the same scale as the Community market, and thus there is room for no more than one, two, or at a maximum, three European firms (the building of computers, the aircraft industry, the building of nuclear reactors, and tomorrow, perhaps, the manufacture of oceanographic equipment).

There are only a small number of possible approaches to take in proceeding with the necessary reorganization of these industries. Either the existing European firms could each associate with an American firm: in effect, this would be a case of takeover (of the kind of buying-in used with Bull by General Electric, and then by Honeywell). In this case, there is no longer a European decision-making center in this field. Or within one country, a regrouping of national firms could lead to the setting-up of a firm of international dimension. Such an operation might arouse suspicion among other countries and drive several governments to promote the setting-up of competing national firms.

Or last, the problem could be tackled at the Community level, from the outset, on a plurisectoral basis, which alone could permit compensations. Agreement would thus be reached on promoting the birth of a certain number of European companies, each built around a nucleus provided by a firm in one country but having establishments in several Community countries (and, eventually, in nonmember countries). In a way, this would amount to facilitating the birth of European multinational companies.

The third way is certainly not simple, but we must know what we want: efficiency can be acquired while losing independence (the first approach); independence vis-a-vis nonmember countries can be preserved by sacrificing efficiency (the second approach); but only with the third approach can we hope to attain independence and efficiency at the same time.

What has first been said for sectoral structures is valid, mutatis mutandis, for large scientific and technological operations, with the difference that the second approach is often barred. It is even probable that the most profitable results would be yielded by pooling the entire Community's resources in scientific and technical research activities. It is certainly not being suggested here to organize everything at the Community level: the biggest part of public expenditure must continue to be directed at the national level by means of a certain mutual exchange of information. But working jointly becomes necessary where the scope of the effort needed to obtain profitable results exceeds the financial means of one country (for basic research, when very large equipment if necessary, and for various industrial sectors, such as the nuclear, space, data-processing, and aircraft industries; urban or suburban transportation; and oceanography).

This is also necessary where the products are put to use in setting up networks (as in telecommunications—including teleprocessing). Finally, it should be applied where the competition between firms in different countries is slight and where the pooling of efforts would make possible great economies and a saving of time (housing, savings in energy, and so forth).

Harmonization of Macroeconomic Policies

Everyone agrees on the inadequacy of the customs union and the Common Market in its present form, as well as the need for a real economic and monetary union. There is also a fairly general consensus on the ultimate goals at which to aim: monetary union (either currencies irrevocably welded together or, even better, a single currency); harmonization of economic policies; and a single decision-making center in the Community.

The present state of things, as we have seen, is far off the mark: (1) price evolutions differ from country to country; (2) even if the principle of fixed exchange parities has been accepted and a short-term commitment has been made to maintaining them through the "Snake", the idea has also been accepted that they may be adjusted from time to time, and several currencies remain outside the "Snake"; (3) the dollar is still the most used currency for intra-Community commercial transactions; and (4) economic policies are more related than harmonized.

How can the current state of things be guided toward the achievement of the desirable final goals?

The present difficulties and those foreseeable for the near future come from the fact that price evolutions are different from one country to the next, as well as from economic factors (such as different ratios of increase in productivities and the different sensitivity of raw materials to world prices), which result in different kinds of political behavior. The basic problem, therefore, is to change the kinds of behavior: it is not enough to ask governments to agree on the rates of increase in prices and products (as was the case in the Third Medium-Term Program); these agreements, even if sincere, will certainly fall apart if the behavior of various national economic agents cannot be changed and made more compatible at the Community level. Thus, a twofold choice must be made: one choice between three possible strategies—one strategy based on exchange, another exclusively economic, and the third, mixed—and another choice between two concepts—a progressive alignment by small steps or an abrupt advance in one or a small number of jumps.

The strategy based on exchange would consist in immediately deciding on a very strict timetable of stages, which would lead to a complete rigidity in exchange rates. It might thus be decided that parity adjustments could be made for a limited period of time, with a margin that would decrease annually until totally eliminated.

This is a tempting notion, all the more so since it seems to have a precedent in the stage-by-stage elimination of customs duties. But this is largely a fallacious analogy. Trade movements are subject to considerable inertia, whereas capital movements are easy and fast by nature, whenever no obstacles are put in their way. And the balance of payments between countries with different rates of price increases can only be equilibrated, if changes in the exchange rates are excluded, by capital movements. A strategy essentially based on exchange, therefore, runs the risk of leading to sizable capital movements, as well as to unemployment in some regions. In the long run, according to the classical pattern, there would be pressure on the prices in the country where they increased the most, but this adjustment would only take place after some time and at the cost of disturbances—particularly unemployment—which must be considered unacceptable.[*] Thus, this strategy based on exchange is inapplicable— at least in its pure form.

On the other hand, emphasis might be placed mainly on coordinating economic policies, and those efforts might be intensified that have so far been inadequate. On bringing closer the characteristics of the various countries' economic evolutions, the reasons for exchange modifications could slowly be made to disappear. Thus, after time, there would be a real stability in exchange rates, which would only have to be given official recognition, for example, by introducing a common currency. Putting such a strategy into effect would necessitate the following measures: (1) instituting an enormous survey and research program; (2) strengthening and increasing the consultations between those in power (including the representatives of the social partners); and (3) the progressive setting-up of a Community decision-making center.

This strictly economic proceeding, as important as it would be, would still be inadequate in some ways. On one hand, the lack of any control over movements of floating capital lets troubles develop (that become more and more unacceptable). On the other hand, it would be a shame to do without the additional assistance that might be hoped for from a decision taken concerning exchanges: any measure that could reassure economic agents against the risk of changes in the exchange rate should usually promote trade and make spontaneous behavior more "Community" in nature, something which, in the long run, could bring the evolution of the different economies closer together.

Thus, we are led to consider a mixed strategy, which was, moreover, the one approved at the Paris Summit Conference: "The Heads of State or Government have reaffirmed the principle of parallel progress in the different fields of economic and monetary union."

Progress in the coming years will be made by putting simultaneously into effect the two groups of measures described above: a

_____

[*] This is indeed the opinion of the Community's Monetary Committee.

more and more intensified coordination of economic policies and a
greater and greater rigidity of exchange rates, plus additional measures taken in relation to the outside world.

Strictly monetary measures are meant to neutralize the effects
of temporary factors, which may make it difficult to maintain parities.
Some progress was made in this direction by setting up the Monetary
Cooperation Fund, but its allocations are inadequate. Similarly,
coordination of the monetary measures taken by national authorities
will have to be strengthened. Finally, the pooling of gold and foreign
currency reserves could be accomplished by successive stages, rather
than being carried out in one step at the moment of moving into the
final state.

While awaiting the reform of the international monetary system,
the Community has adopted a joint floating approach vis-a-vis the
outside world. This was one of the possible ways to ward off disturbances coming from the outside; the alternative would have consisted
in setting up a real checkpoint of foreign exchanges at the Community's
frontiers—which could have then made it possible to subject the
Eurodollars in side to the (now lacking) public regulation. We may
wonder if, in the coming years, we will not be led to have recourse
to both measures simultaneously; everything will depend on how
quickly an international solution is adopted, as well as on the form
it takes.

Finally, one may wonder if it would not be better to create
a Community currency right away. Obviously, it is a paradoxical
situation that the Nine, who carry out half their total foreign trade
with each other, use for this the currency of a country with which
they have six times less trade. It is even more paradoxical if the
Community currencies float vis-a-vis this outside currency.

A Community unit of account already exists, which is defined
as a weighted average of the various national currencies. First,
this currency could be used for the transactions of the central banks,
but it is to be desired that it will gradually become a currency of
exchange, and then an instrument of payment. In order to achieve
that, it will have to be attractive enough so that economic operaters
will gradually come to prefer it to the dollar. But it would be beyond
the scope of this book to go into the corresponding technical details.

As for the speed this progression should take, the lessons of
the years 1968-76—described in Chapter 4—seem very clear: the
step-by-step approach, where only the most urgent problem is
tackled and the next crisis is awaited before making another step,
has demonstrated its ineffectiveness; it is not a series of crises that
is going to push the partners to make the necessary concessions.
Solutions must be adopted, without emotion, before the problems
become crucial; this obviously presupposes a political willpower,
which we will speak about again in the concluding chapter.

Community Solidarity

The very notion of "Community" implies putting into effect a
certain solidarity between the members of this Community. Although
it is not stressed, this idea appears in the Treaty: "Anxious to
strengthen the unity of their economies and to ensure their harmonious
development by reducing the differences existing between the various
regions and the backwardness of the less favored regions. . . "

But the awkward question is: To whose benefit should this solidarity work, and how far should it go? Without a doubt, a total solidarity in all things at the Community level cannot be expected now,
yet it would be unfair to ask for a marriage only "for better." Should,
therefore, some of the ideas of solidarity that exist at the national
level be brought to the Community level? Should new Community
ideas of solidarity be introduced?

Bringing the different ideas of national solidarity to the Community level might be interpreted either as aligning national systems
or as a system of a Community budget redistribution of the resources
contributed. Neither of these actions need be absolutely necessary.
Differences in national concepts and practices reflect the different
ways of thinking of the peoples of the Community, and there is no
reason to try to reduce them. However, it is likely that the spontaneous drawing closer that has occurred (see Chapter 3) will continue
in the future.[*] As for working through a Community budget, that
would only weigh things down more.

Although it hardly seems useful to bring to the Community level—
at least on a large scale—those solidarities already in effect at the
national level, on the other hand, defining and implementing new
ideas of solidarity to come into play on a Community scale must
naturally follow the working out of a European union. Thus, true
Community social and regional policies must be defined.

Regarding social policy, a major step was taken, as was seen,
in reforming the Social Fund. In its present form, it could result
in a considerable redistribution to the benefit of those countries
experiencing a particularly intense process of adjustment of their
labor force. Since 1975, in fact, the Community budget has been
maintained by its own resources, and the actual contribution of each
national economy is thus based on its GNP and the volume of its
imports coming from nonmember countries, whereas the allocations

---

[*] The fear of losing their autonomy with regard to social
systems—and even more their life style—accounts, in part, for the
Norwegians' refusal to join the Community.

of the Social Fund are related to the scope of the programs of labor
readaptation carried out in each country.*

At present, the Community has at its disposal five financial
instruments for intervening directly in regional economies: the
Regional Fund, the EAGGF, the Social Fund, the ECSC funds, and
the European Investment Bank. A certain number of other actions m
may have considerable impact. Thus, it is beginning to develop
the coordination procedures that are, for the moment, still very
inadequate.

Moreover, this same problem exists on a wider basis for all
the elements of the Community budget, whose elaboration, along
with that of the Medium-Term Economic Program, could provide an
opportunity to check the consistency of Community actions as a
whole—which does not mean that the budget must be substantially
increased. †

Nonmember Countries: A Policy

The international context has changed dramatically since the
time the European treaties were signed. It has moved from a bipolarity to a multipolarity. Thus, European relations with the rest of
the world must be completely reconsidered, whether with Western
industrialized countries, Eastern countries, or developing countries.

From the economic standpoint, the Community's attitude will
depend on what answer it comes up with to this basic question: What
degree of liberalization is acceptable—or, conversely, what degree
of public control of external economic relations is necessary—to
enable the Community to shape its identity and establish that European
Union which the Paris Summit Conference said should be accomplished
"before the end of the present decade."

First, it should be remarked that the idea of liberalization in
no way contradicts the resolve to open outward, which has been so

----

* Along with this increase in the activity of the Social Fund,
the Social Action Program forwarded to the Council by the Commission
in October 1973 included many proposals that centered on full and
better employment, an improvement in living and working conditions,
and participation of the social partners in Community decisions.

† The budget for 1977 is slightly over 9 billion ua, that is, 7
percent of the Community product and 3 percent of all public expenditure within the Community—65 percent goes to the EAGGF, 7 percent to the Social Fund, 5 percent to the Regional Fund, and 6 percent to operating expenses.

often voiced (and reaffirmed in the Paris declaration). On one hand, history teaches us that economic unions and federalized states have always been formed from within—and protected—by a border barrier. This was as true for the United States (which, as a matter of fact, followed a rather strong protectionist line for some time) as for the Germany of the Zollverein (the customs union of the nineteenth century). On the other hand, a thorough opening up to the outside is only conceivable in a spirit of reciprocity and mutual benefit. Thus, it is automatically limited in a world where there are so many economic barriers protecting nonmember countries and where the monetary framework leaves so much to be desired—it particularly lets sources of short-term disequilibria function; thus, by its very nature, it brings into play a disequilibrium that benefits one economy in relation to the others.

The extent to which exchanges should be free must be established for goods, persons, and capital.

For goods, customs protection is now very slight, and thus, new reductions must apply to nontariff obstacles.

During these negotiations, it is important that the Community see that those instruments are kept which are useful for putting a real industrial policy into effect. Much as it seems natural to avoid putting up new obstacles to trade if the partners avoid this as well, so would it be foolhardy to throw aside in the name of free trade those means of action necessary for redirecting production structures. This is why a very definite industrial policy should be worked out before proceeding with this trade negotiation. The delay resulting from the necessarily long GATT negotiations should be used for a complete reconsideration of the Community's industrial structures and of the specializations that should be promoted to profit the utmost from the trade advantages. In this, we must take into account the requirements of independence and the possibility of letting some activities traditionally located in Europe be shifted to the developing countries (extrapolating—to other countries and industries—on the basis of Great Britain's decision a few years ago to substantially cut back its textile industry).

This same need to couple industrial policy and foreign policy exists for the movements of workers coming from nonmember countries. Currently, about 7 percent of the wage-earners in the Community of Nine are immigrant workers, and this rate increases every year. The Community, therefore, cannot do without an immigration policy, which must simultaneously take into account economic, social, and political considerations.

Immigrants fulfill certain tasks that are considered too difficult or too unpleasant by the European population; the alternative to using their labor would be either to set up a kind of civic service

requiring all Europeans to spend a certain amount of time working
at these tasks or to radically change working techniques, automating
the most difficult tasks. From a social standpoint, the European
countries must considerably improve the conditions in which these
immigrant workers are received and live, conditions that often border
on the scandalous. Finally, these movements of workers coming from
nonmember countries, whether these countries are Mediterranean
or in other continents, should be integrated into the policy of relations
with the developing countries: both the flows to these countries coming
from wages earned in Europe and the training that at least some of
these immigrants receive, and which they can use if they return home,
constitute a contribution to the less developed countries. Both these
and the industrialized countries may find it in their interest to maintain the population movements, provided that these are organized in
the threefold interest of the home countries, the host countries, and
the immigrants themselves. It is urgent for the Community to work
out an immigration policy that consistently takes into account all of
these aspects, since no country has yet worked out such a policy.

Lastly, capital movements raise very different problems,
depending on whether they are long-term direct investments or short-
term speculative investments.

The Community discussions on the first type of flow have been
almost nonexistent. But the Community cannot keep on eluding a
problem that becomes more and more important each day. Of course,
in Europe, we are still a long way from the situation existing in
Canada, where:

> The great and increasing foreign stranglehold—especially
> American—on Canadian economic activity has given
> birth to an industrial structure which largely reflects
> the growth priorities of foreign firms. . . . Canada
> finds itself prisoner of a system of innovation and tech-
> nological development which is remote-controlled from
> abroad. . . . This development has helped integrate
> Canada into the world economy in a way which could
> make it more difficult for us to reach our growth
> and employment objectives. [2]

Yet, the Canadian diagnosis is interesting to the extent that it
can put us on our guard and enable us to react in time. In order to
give shape to the moderate reaction that is necessary, the advantages
brought by direct foreign investments in Europe, for instance, in the
form of a transfer of advanced technology (including the field of
management), and the drawbacks connected to them, particularly
regarding a reduction in the Community's autonomy in accomplishing

its development objectives, both quantitative and qualitative, should
be compared. Only such a concrete study will make it possible to
work out an effective strategy and prevent giving way to emotional
impulses.

For movements of floating capital, which have no advantages
at all (and considerable disadvantages) for the economy in general,
there is an undeniable need for immediate action. The only uncertainty
lies in not knowing whether the reform of the monetary system will
be quick enough and broad enough to solve the problem or if, at least
temporarily, the Community should take measures on its own. It is
difficult to see how these measures could take any form other than
a degree of control over foreign exchanges at the Community's borders
and submitting Eurodollars to the normal regulations that govern
credit (and, thus, these regulations should themselves undergo a
certain harmonization between member countries).

List of Priorities

The various tasks just listed are obviously not independent
of each other, and the order in which they should be carried out is
important. Here, we will not try to lay out a real action program
with a timetable but will offer, instead, a few general observations
on some economic, social, and political connections.

From an economic standpoint, one must distinguish between
operations related to the completion of the Common Market and
structural operations that encompass much more. Actions such as
the elimination of technical hindrances to trade and the liberalization
of movements of those in the liberal professions (doctors, and so forth)
are useful in the sense that they get rid of various sources of waste or
inefficiency. Everything that may lead to a reduction in costs and
an equalizing of the marginal efficiency of the production factors is,
a priori, beneficial and should be sought. But we must not fool
ourselves: the largest results are no longer to be expected there;
most of that harvest is already in.

Of far greater importance is what might lead firms to think
in terms of a single economic area and to make their decisions in
that light. In this regard, there are two decisive factors: eliminating
the borders constituted by different tax systems, which presupposes
a major alignment of indirect taxes, and establishing the rigidity of
exchange rates between member countries' currencies.

However, the reorganization of firms is also often influenced
by public decisions. Thus, it is imperative that there be a systematic
correlation, much more than has so far been the case, among
various policies: there should be correlation of competition

policy and the supervision mentioned in Article 92 over public aids; and regional policy, which favors the various sectors unequally, depending on whether the development of the infrastructure is stressed (very favorable to some heavy industries, such as harbor installations for the steel industry) or direct subsidies to create jobs (more useful for light industries); as well as employment policy through the Social Fund; immigration policy; foreign policy—as much by the specializations that it encourages in developing countries as by the security considerations it must take into account; and scientific and technical research policy. If we keep on treating these policies as separate, we will increase the inconsistencies to the detriment of us all.

This in no way means that the policies as a whole should be decided on at the Community level. Centralization is often costly and slow. The double temptation to want to see everything standardized and brought to the Community level must be resisted. Thus, what is to be decided and carried out at the Community level must be carefully selected, making sure that the action has a good chance of being more effective at this level than at the national or intranational level. In this way, some operations where Community action will replace national action, as well as some operations where Community action will complete the national actions, will be undertaken. For those actions accompanying or complementing national actions, it is important to make sure they will not simply take over from the national actions, which will then disappear. But we must avoid recreating situations like that of the former system of the Social Fund, whereby each country received as much as it had contributed, and, therefore, there was no additional action in favor of reconversion. The best way to avoid this—probably the only way—is to require that Community actions be decided upon only in relation to the drawing up of coordinated national programs. If this requirement is respected, the extension of Community actions will probably be slowed down but will be made more effective.

Finally, harmonizing macroeconomic policies is particularly urgent. Without this, the member countries' currencies cannot be finally welded together. As long as the countries continue to consider the manipulating of the exchange rates an an instrument of external adjustment, there remains a risk that the Community might break up, or, at the least, retrogress toward a vague free trade area, without forming a real European industrial fabric.

However, all that has preceded is from the realm of cold logic. But the progression in European construction is not an end in itself; it must come from the aspirations of the various populations. For that to happen, each group of citizens must have the feeling that it has something to gain from this construction, in standards of living, in working conditions, in stability and security, and in the fulfillment of its deepest hopes.

Therefore, the Community should have a complete social policy which is not merely a complement to other community policies, but which can become a real state of mind drawing inspiration from all the other accomplishments. All actions should be made to converge on the road to a better European society; this point will be returned to later.

Lastly, Europe is developing in a highly evolving international contest. The resolve to open outward is fundamental. Europe must not draw into itself; even if it wanted to, it could not. But this idea of opening up can be conceived of in an active or passive aspect. In the ideal world of the classical economic theory of international trade, it is carried out on the basis of the compared advantages of Ricardo, and each gains from international specialization. Two basic differences separate this theory from reality: the lack of any policy of international competition that neutralizes the tendencies to mono-polistic behavior and government interference in international econo-mic exchanges. It may be regretted, but the result is that external supply cannot be considered as safe as internal supply, for prices as well as for quantities; therefore, trade agreements always remain an important instrument of foreign policy—and, thus, Europe cannot do without an overall conception of its economic and political relations with the rest of the world. It has been shown that this has been one of the areas where progress has been the slowest.

To sum up, there are two possible approaches for continuing European construction. In one, Community actions would be very restricted:

1. The harmonization would be reduced to the bare minimum that is necessary to the healthy functioning of the Common Market; it would be concerned with technical points (such as the truck axle load and a few rules regarding pollution), taxes (such as the general basis of assessment of the tax used to maintain the Community budget) and regulatory matters (texts concerning insurance and banks).

2. Currencies would not be welded together; instead, the possi-bility would be left open to turn to changes in the exchange rate, but attempts would be made to keep these changes with certain limits, which would probably lead them to be rather frequent. (Here, inspira-tion would be drawn from the so-called crawling peg technique.) At the same time, efforts would be made to make national economic policies as consistent as possible.

3. There would practically be no policy of industrial structures; the development of these structures would be left totally to the discre-tion of the firms, except for possibly a few interventions made on behalf of industries with particular difficulties.

4. Community "solidarity" would be limited to some redistri-bution of resources, more especially by way of the Regional Fund.

Generally, this conception would be broadly based on the idea of a free trade area, but modernized and constituted to keep national policies from trying to oppose each other (overbidding on subsidies, beggar my neighbor policy, and so forth).

The second approach is far more ambitious:

1. First, without becoming overly perfectionist, a serious effort would be made to get rid of the main obstacles to the free movement of goods and production factors.

2. Special attention would be paid to aligning indirect tax rates, with a view to eliminating the tax cordon at the internal borders.

3. By choosing a very limited number of points of impact, based on a comparison of national policies, a guiding Community action would be brought to bear on industrial structures.

4. There would be as rapid a movement as possible toward making intra-Community exchange rates rigid, such a step having been made possible by a thorough coordination of economic policies. This implies common objectives but does not mean that the measures would have to be the same in all countries.

5. There would be rather broad Community solidarity, but there would also be careful supervision to make sure that Community budgeted expenditure led to the desired objectives and brought about transfers to certain regions or to certain categories of inhabitants and were not simply transfers between nations.

6. The Community as such would define a real attitude vis-a-vis the rest of the world, whether in questions of aid to developing countries, of the international division of labor between industrialized countries, of the supervision of multinational firms, or of ensuring the availability of supplies of strategic products.

The above conception is linked to the formation of a European political union.

The first approach, which might be symbolized in the formula OECD plus Regional Fund, is clearly a retreat in comparison with the Treaty of Rome, and even in comparison with the Six's earlier accomplishments. It rather broadly reflects the viewpoints of many British circles, who dislike the idea of committing themselves further, at least for the time being. Their attitude can be explained by the history of the British economy over the last 25 years. This history has been marked by a series of periods of slow growth and attempts at rapid expansion, which were abruptly halted by serious deficits in the balance of payments (the stop-and-go policy). The overriding concern has been to keep in the hands of the government all the levers that make it possible to ensure external equilibrium; this goes very well with their wish to transfer as little as possible to institutions that are not purely British.

The second approach goes beyond the letter of the Rome Treaty, without, however, necessitating any amendments. It reflects the views expressed at the Paris and the Hague Summit conferences, and it is shared by many circles on the continent who have the experience of the Common Market behind them and who have become convinced that if the people involved restrict themselves to a minimalist course of action, they will not see the European Union take on its full economic effectiveness nor see Europe return to a role of major political importance in world affairs.

Yet, if this second approach is to be applied, even spread out over several years, it requires an adequate institutional organization and unfaltering political willpower.

In the declaration made at the 1972 Paris Summit Conference: "The Heads of State and Government found that the Community institutions were proving themselves, but considered that the decision procedures and the running of the Institutions ought to be improved to boost their efficiency."

In essence, it is a matter of improving and speeding up the decision-making mechanism, of strengthening the democratic control of this mechanism, and of organizing the new Community decision-making centers necessary for the working of the Economic and Monetary Union, as argued in the Vedel report.

Time has proved the effectiveness of the highly original decision-making system developed by the Treaty of Rome, which is based on associating the Council and the Commission: "The Commission represents the strictly common interest in those fields open to Community action; the Council incarnates the political resolve and the cooperation of the various States, joining together to accomplish the Community tasks." But, in practice, the fundamental institutional balance between these two organs has undergone a slight change: there is an increased predominance of the Council; unanimity has replaced majority vote in Council decisions since the Luxembourg compromise of January 1966; and new organs have appeared that were not provided for in the Treaty—the Permanent Representatives Committee (which draws up the Council's decisions), administration committees (particularly for implementing agricultural policy), and, finally, summit conferences. Thus, the Community institutions have changed their nature to a degree. Not only has the intergovernmental character of the Council been increased, but this quality has been carried down to lower Community authorities and been reproduced in mechanisms that tend to develop outside the Community. The Commission has not been affected by this process, but because of the increasing limitations placed on its role, it risks being reduced to a mere administrative, if not technocratic, function. The result of this has been a slowdown in the decision-making process, as well as a certain risk of inconsistency in the various actions undertaken.

To remedy this, the top-heaviness of the Council must be reduced and the Council must place more confidence in the Commission and delegate its authority to it. Majority rule must be readopted for most decisions, and the Council must devote less of its time to problems of secondary importance, thus enabling it to deal more broadly and thoroughly with those subjects most vital to the development of the Community.

Developing common policies demands the transfer of new decision-making powers to Community institutions. The transfers called for by the Werner report in monetary matters are only one example out of many. But there is an accompanying danger, which the Vedel report clearly points out:

> On the eve of a closer cooperation between the Member
> States which will lead them well beyond the customs union
> to the formation of an Economic and Monetary Union
> and to developing common policies in fields other
> than agriculture, a two-fold danger must be stressed,
> which threatens both the effectiveness and the democratic
> nature of the development in sight: firstly, the tendency
> to interpret Community jurisdiction in a too restrictive
> fashion; and, secondly, the proliferation of intergo-
> vernmental organs and committees on the fringes of
> the Community's institutional framework. The cohesion
> of European policy as a whole will be threatened.
> Moreover, the provisions of the Treaty will be under-
> mined by by-passing Parliamentary and jurisdictional
> control, the elements necessary to every democratic
> legal system. [3]

The conclusion is quite clear: "If it proves to be necessary to form new committees of high ranking national civil servants, these committees must be fit into the Community structure and be linked to both the Council and the Commission in the manner provided for the Monetary Committee." [4]

However, every increase in Community tasks, responsibilities, and powers makes it more and more necessary to strengthen demo-cratic control and thus to increase the authority of Parliament. It has been proposed that the latter take part in choosing the president of the Commission, that it share decision-making power in some cases and be consulted in others, and, finally, that it play a larger role in adopting the budget. But all that will only take on its true importance the day Parliament is elected by universal suffrage and when, in European public opinion, the Parliament is a crucial body in the running of the Community (so that persons of some political stature will come forward and present their candidacy). The election of deputies to the European Parliament by universal suffrage will take place for the first time in 1978. This is an event that could be of capital importance for the development of the Community.

Thus, institutional development forms a whole within which internal coherence must be maintained, particularly by keeping within the Community framework and avoiding the formation of parallel frameworks that may more or less quickly become competitors, to the detriment of the overall effectiveness.

NOTES

1. EEC Commission, Exposé des motifs des Propositions de directives en matière de droits d'accise.

2. Herbert Gray (Canadian revenue minister), Report, May 1971.

3. Rapport du groupe ad hoc pour l'examen du problème de l'accroissement des compétences du Parlement européen (Rapport Vedel) (1972).

4. EEC, Article 105.

CONCLUSION:
THE PRIMACY OF
POLITICS

During the period covered in this survey of the first years of
the Common Market, European construction neither stands out as
the great epic of the twentieth century nor as a collapsing myth but
far more as a vast, unfinished building project—one whose final
appearance and usefulness its builders are wondering about today.

In too many Community discussions, the Community authorities
act as if there can be a winner only if there is a loser; they reason
as if they were taking part in a zero sum game, whereas European
construction is worthwhile because it is a positive sum game, which
allows everyone to win. Only if it yields a net gain is a new course
of action or a new step ahead justified.

The Community field, therefore, should be the perfect one for
carrying out studies to weigh the advantages and drawbacks of various
approaches, bringing out the positive balance of the proposals for
the Community and the repercussions for the various categories of
agents concerned. Only on the basis of such analyses can "package
deals" acceptable to all be worked out, because everyone would gain.

But assessing these advantages and drawbacks—and their
balance—presupposes that reference will be made to some idea of
development in the medium and the long term. It is this idea that
at present is most lacking in the Community. The Community has
not known what type of society it wanted to work toward; it has had
no overall long-term framework into which it might fit each of the
actions it contemplated, and it has not been able to see clearly what
benefit could be drawn from a joint advance into a future that remains
undefined. In such circumstances, it has not been able to avoid a
certain Balkanization and a dispersal of its actions, as a result of
which there has not been sufficient coherence between both national
and Community activities and the various activities undertaken by
the Community itself. Admittedly, there have been many proposals,
but to some extent, this has occurred because the absence of any
clear vision of a long-term objective has prevented the day-to-day
priorities from being strictly defined.

Not that this phenomenon is peculiar to the Community; all
countries exhibit an absence of long-term strategy. A striking
illustration is to be found in the vicissitudes of medium-term planning,
both in countries that have been practicing it for as long as a quarter
of a century and in those only seeking to introduce it. This lack of any
clear view on long-term development is not confined to political
institutions but can also be seen in varying degrees in other institutions.

inherently less subject to contingencies, such as the universities and the churches. Paradoxical as it may seem, it is in the multinational companies that the tendency to formulate and operate a long-term strategy appears to be most marked. It is paradoxical because the difficulties of arguing about a distant horizon might seem all the greater if the field of action is more diverse; but the paradox is only apparent, for this diversity of situations in different fields and different countries in which the companies operate opens the way to compensation and introduces flexibility into the operation of strategy.

The Community institutions also have to carry out activities in a great variety of fields and in different countries. If they are to be able to work out such a strategy, they will have to develop joint study of the great problems of Europe 10 or 15 years ahead and arrive at practical conclusions for both national and Community action. It will then be possible to concentrate more on the problems of tomorrow than on those of today, on the creation of something new rather than on the harmonization of what already exists.

This working out of a common vision of the kind of European society to be created is, in its very nature, a political task; first, there must be some careful groundwork done by experts, emphasizing the foreseeable problems and their possible solutions and, then, laying out several possible courses to be followed. But the course chosen must be the outcome of the democratic process, bringing together all the living forces of the nations of Europe—economic, social, and political.

Thus, only when a "master plan" is defined that is capable of rallying supporters and of galvanizing a certain enthusiasm will Europe again be able to mobilize the ardor and effort of its inhabitants.

The choice is probably much more urgent than many Europeans (who are bogged down in their partisan squabbles) think.

Whether political "Europe" comes into being or not is probably only moderately important as far as economic efficiency goes: each European country is now too small to be able to draw into itself for very long or to break the economic bonds it has built with its neighbors. The Common Market, in the limited sense of a free trade area, is irreversible. But the outcome could be greatly different as regards the way of life, and it is in this that several courses offer themselves as possibilities.

In following one of these courses, the Europeans could continue their mutual distrust and their sacred egotism. They may react to every severe shock by protecting their immediate personal interests. The tutelage of Uncle Sam, in this case, will grow, just tactfully enough not to rouse the worries of their Russian neighbor, but completely enough so that, after a generation, the European personality will have totally abdicated before the "American way of life," and

Europe will no longer have anything to say in world affairs. The prophecy Paul Valéry made in 1938 will come true: "Europe is ready to be governed by an American Commission.

Following an alternative course, the Europeans could show a burst of energy starting today: realizing that it is to their interest— and that of the world—to have a "European way" of economic and social development, they could take their own destiny in hand once again and agree to make the necessary efforts. Europeans must make efforts to secure their own defense, acting together in such a way that the richest countries help those countries that are less well-off, and make mutual concessions in accepting a degree of specialization of production. This means that each country must abandon certain products and give up the illusion of independence in order to reach an agreement on a single foreign policy. Such concessions are necessary to set up a true European union, where each nation, moreover, is able to keep its own character to the extent that it permits agreement on the major decisions to be taken, and particularly on Europe's role in the world.

Might a third possible course be possible, where the European population, starting out to follow the first course, would kick over the traces, after 10 or 15 years, with the encouragement of China? It is to be feared that the great burst of energy would be futile and that Europe would no longer be able to recover its integrity. Furthermore, without righting long-term developments, this reaction could seriously disturb economic activity and political equilibrium for several years: thus, here we would lose at every level.

Europe no longer has much time to make its choice.

Nothing is completely lost, but it is always later than one thinks.

SELECTED BIBLIOGRAPHY

COMMISSION PUBLICATIONS

Community life is regularly described in the General Report of the Activities of the European Communities, which the Commission presents to the Europe Parliament every February, and in the Bulletin of the European Communities (issued monthly with supplements). In addition to the General Report, there is each year an account of the social situation within the Community; since 1972, there has been a report on competition policy, and since 1975, a report on the agricultural situation in the Community.

The Commission also publishes various studies in different series, particularly the Economy and Finance and Competition series.

Related to subjects dealt with in this book, the following reports may also be noted:

The First, Second, Third and Fourth Medium-Term Economic Program.
The Plan Mansholt 1969 (agricultural policy).
La Politique industrielle de la Communauté (1970).
Rapport au Conseil et à la Commission concernant la réalisation par étapes de l'Union économique et monétaire dans la Communauté (Rapport Werner) (1970).
La politique monétaire dans les pays de la C.E.E. (1972).
Rapport du groupe ad hoc pour l'examen du probleme de l'accroissement des compétences du Parlement européen (Rapport Vedel) (1972).
L'Union Européenne (Rapport Tindemans) (1976).

Lastly, the Statistical Office of the European Communities publishes enormous general collections of comparable statistics (in particular, a yearbook of the different governments' national accounting)

The official decisions of the Community institutions are published in the Official Journal of the European Communities. These publications can be obtained from the European Community Information Service, 2100 M Street, NW, Suite 707, Washington D.C. 20037, or from the Office for Official Publications of the European Communities, in Luxembourg.

OTHER WORKS

Allais, Maurice. L'Europe unie—route de la prospérité. Paris:
Calmann-Levy, 1960.

Arnaud-Amelier, Paule. Europe: vers une politique conjoncturelle
commune. Paris: A. Colin.

Balassa, Bela. The Theory of Economic Integration. London: Allen
and Unwin, 1961.

Cairncross, Alec, ed. Economic Policy for the European Community:
The Way Forward. London: McMillan, 1974.

Clerc, Francois. Le Marché Commun agricole. PUF, collection
"Que sais-je?" 5th ed. 1973.

Deniau, J. F. Le March Commun. PUF, collection "Que sais-je?"
11th ed. 1974.

Denton, Geoffrey R., ed. Economic Integration in Europe.
Weidenfeld & Nicolson, 1969.

—, ed. Economic and Monetary Union in Europe. Croom Helm for
the Federal Trust, 1975.

Flory, Jean, and Toulemon, Robert. Une politique industrielle pour
l'Europe. PUF, coll. "SUP." 1974.

Hallstein, Walter. Europe in the Making. London: Allen & Unwin,
1973.

Leroy, Pierre. L'avenir du Marché Commun Agricole. Presses
Universitaires de France, "SUP." collection 1973.

Meade, J. E. The Theory of Customs Unions. Amsterdam: North
Holland Publishing Co., 1955.

Pinder, John, ed. The Economics of Europe (What the Common
Market Means for Britian). London: Charles Knight, 1971.

Salin, Pascal, ed. l'unification monétaire européenne. Paris:
Calmann-Lévy, 1974.

Sampson, Anthony. The New Europeans. Hodder & Stoughton, 1968.

Scitovsky, Tibor. Economic Theory and Western European Integration.
Stanford, Calif.: Stanford University Press, 1958.

Taber, George. Patterns and Prospects of Common Market Trade.
Peter Owen, 1974.

Tinbergen, Jan. International Economic Integration. Amsterdam:
Elsevier, 1954.

Twitchett, Kenneth J., ed. Europe in the World. Europa Publications,
1976.

Lastly, the Revue du Marché Commum (Paris) and The Journal of
Common Market Studies (Blackwell Publishers) deal with many
different subjects.

52
(4)